FIX
FRUSTRATIONS
AT WORK

*Short Stories Empowering
You to Make the Difference*

Kent C. Porter

INDIE BOOKS
INTERNATIONAL

ISBN: 1-941870-57-0
ISBN 13: 978-1-941870-57-0
Library of Congress Control Number: 2016939833

Designed by Joni McPherson, mcphersongraphics.com

INDIE BOOKS INTERNATIONAL, LLC
2424 VISTA WAY, SUITE 316
OCEANSIDE, CA 92054
www.indiebooksintl.com

To all the heroes and heroines in these stories who courageously found their voices and overcame their frustrations at work

Please share your comments and how you fixed your frustrations.

Kent Porter
Tel: (858) 692-0438
Email: kent@porterleadership.com

Contents

....

Preface

....

You Are a Difference Maker

You are a difference maker. But you may not be in touch with how you currently are making a difference.

Has anyone ever said anything to you that was uplifting, brightened your day, changed the way you see things, or even changed your life?

The answer has to be yes. So that person is a difference maker; that person made a difference. It wasn't a headline-making difference, but it made a difference to you. In some cases, it was just the right gesture or just the right comment at just the right time.

Have you ever said something or done something for someone that you forgot about, and were surprised when they told you it was uplifting, brightened their day, or put a smile on their face?

Your answer has to be yes. You are a difference maker.

We think in terms of big or noteworthy differences, while dismissing a comment that lightened a burden, created a smile, or gave hope.

Recognize you can make a difference, where you are, every day. Difference-making not only lifts up others, it elevates you.

Making a difference should be your every-day purpose. Purpose transcends you, changes your behavior, and gives meaning when you most need it.

You can start each day by saying out loud, "I am a difference maker." Why out loud? Because we believe our own voice.

Expect better relationships, less tension, and perhaps a promotion. The difference maker is one example of how being proactive can soften and fix your frustrations.

What to Expect

What follows are thirty-two short stories to empower you to make work better and more enjoyable. As you read a story, visualize what you can become by applying what you read. Each is a story of personal struggle and ultimate success and takes about ten minutes to read. They are stories about real people fixing themselves by learning how to fix difficult and stressful situations with their bosses and coworkers.

The stories are a distillation of my thirty years of combined experience as a corporate executive, an entrepreneur, and a Board Certified Coach with over 10,000 hours of research into frustrations at work and how others resolved their challenges. My hope is that fixing your frustrations will not only improve your experience at work but also lighten your step and put a smile on your face.

Kent Porter

Subject Index

A Real-Life Miracle

Rob called me up and said, "It's a miracle! I am not exaggerating. I even looked up the definition: 'A highly improbable or extraordinary event that brings very welcome consequences.'"

The Making of a Miracle

His voice was animated and energetic—the antithesis of a week earlier when he had told me he'd followed my advice to talk to Angie from legal about her being a bottleneck on the documentation he needed. My advice hadn't worked.

I'd suggested he sit down with her and try to work out what he could do better on the documentation, and also to find out how much lead time she needed. The meeting had been pleasant, but she was still a bottleneck.

I had previously talked Rob out of going to Angie's boss about her delays because it would send the message to Rob's boss that he couldn't handle difficult conversations, and it would damage his relationship with Angie.

I took a different approach and asked Rob what his attitude was towards Angie. Rob, the hockey fan, told me he had her in his penalty box. In his mind he'd tried to reason, even plead, for cooperation and she'd ignored him.

I asked if he'd spent any time getting to know her and he said he had. He knew she was divorced, had a teenage son who was challenging her authority, and had no family nearby to help.

Rob was sounding more relaxed as we talked so I asked him to tell me some things Angie had done that helped him or others in the company. He said she was patient when explaining legal documents and on occasion helped with personal legal concerns.

Stop Being Judgmental

I told him, "You need an attitude adjustment toward her. You said she's caught up with the documents you needed for the next two weeks, so you have two weeks where you will not be worried about the documents. Use this time to look at what you can do differently, to ponder the concept of judging others and to recognize that even five-year-olds can find fault. You find fault because that is your focus. Stop it.

"Begin by empathizing with raising a teenage boy alone and the challenges she could be facing and the difficulty of not having family nearby to help. Change your focus to look for and expect to see Angie doing good work and helping others.

"During these two weeks find reasons to thank her in person and commend her in public, provided there is a valid reason. Insincerity is easy to spot. Last, concentrate on showing her respect with your tone of voice and body language, and show appreciation."

Results of a Miracle

For two weeks Rob did this, which is why I got the phone call and his declaration of the miraculous event. He struggled to contain himself. "I want to explain what is extraordinary. She hears what I say, and she understands the impact legal delays have on sales and revenues. The average turnaround time from her on my requests was ten days; now it's three and she does it with a smile."

Rob again referenced the definition of miracle: "A highly improbable or extraordinary event that brings very welcome consequences. The miracle within the miracle is my wife commented on how much more positive I was."

ROB'S TAKEAWAYS

- Finding fault is easy. Finding what colleagues, family and friends do well is more effective.

- Stop being judgmental. Start trusting.

- Nagging is not well received; kindness and trust are.

- Creating a miracle is adult fun.

2

Delegation and Life Balance

....

"I'm overwhelmed and scattered. There aren't enough hours in the day." Jason was animated. He continued: "Since my promotion, I'm spending even less time with my wife and two kids."

Good for My Career—Bad for My Family

We talked. Jason told me he delivered on commitments and met deadlines. He saw his promotion as good for his career but found it was bad for his relationship with his family.

He had been told he would have to delegate but found when he did he was disappointed with the results. He decided it was too risky to delegate. He'd set a high bar for himself, which is why he was promoted, but he viewed others as limbo dancers going under the high bar he had set.

I summed things up. "Jason, you told me you get home late and that your family gets the leftovers, that you're an overachiever while others aren't, and you know you should delegate, but won't.

"Sounds like you keep circling around yourself," I said, "and I'd guess this will continue for years."

You Can Complain or Change—It's Your Choice

I ventured forth and said, "You can complain or change. If you want to complain you can talk to a psychologist, but if you want to change, we can talk." I assumed, of course, that he wanted to change, so I asked if he could give me one reason he would commit to change.

Jason's expression changed when he said, "My father died from a heart attack when I was twelve. My children are eight and ten. I want to be around for them."

We deceive ourselves. His reason to change seemed a good one, but was it?

My tough-love alter ego wasn't buying this. I said, "You've been in this job for eighteen months and haven't changed yet. I'll ask the question again. Can you give me one reason—a *good reason*—you will stop doing the work and delegate?"

This question clearly got weightier the longer he took to answer. "I know my problem isn't new. Please give me some insight into what others have done to make a breakthrough."

"My answer may sound overly philosophical," I said, "but it has worked for others. They moved beyond 'it's all about me' to 'it's all about them.' They liked people and found they got out of the prison of fixation on self by helping others."

Reasons to Delegate

After several conversations, I asked Jason to come up with three points that would change his thinking about delegation. These are the bullet points he put on his cell phone and wrote down to put in his wallet.

- To let go is to not control another.
- To let go is to fear less and trust more.
- To let go is to paint a picture of what they can become.

Jason was smart and creative. He knew good intentions weren't enough. He'd need a reminder, so he put a small rock in his shoe—so that when he stood up he'd feel it and remember to check his bullet points. It took him several weeks to memorize them and be able to remove the rock.

He was optimistic about being able to delegate and said he'd talk to his team and would let me know how it went.

Share with Others and You're Forced to Follow Through

A few weeks later Jason called and told me, "I took each of my reports to breakfast and told them I was committed to focusing on their career development. I shared my bullet points and we talked about what each meant to them and to me."

Before the breakfast check came he told each one: "I will be clear in my expectations so when I delegate, you'll be able to get good results 80 percent of the time. And the other 20 percent you'll learn from your mistakes. That's the way I learned. I've got your back. Don't be afraid to make mistakes."

The Proverbial Happy Ending

Soon after this happened Jason surprised his son at a little-league game—the first one he'd ever attended. In baseball parlance, Jason's career had gone from player to player/coach.

His team members felt liberated. They could think for themselves. They felt safe and made decisions, knowing their backs were covered. Being trusted led them to believe they could achieve more.

JASON'S TAKEAWAYS:

- Ask yourself if family and friends get what's left of you after work.

- If they are only getting the leftovers, what can you do differently?

3

The Universal Blind Spot

··

I coached Tom and discussed a comment in his evaluation that said he lacked clarity as to what he wanted to be done on projects. From previous conversations, I knew he valued process, so it was logical to ask, "What is your process for delegation?"

He looked at me as if I had dropped his cell phone in the toilet. "I don't have one," he said with a puzzled look.

I told him I hadn't meant to startle him. "Most people don't have a process. It's a lot like being a parent; one expects to be good at parenting. You expect you'll be good at delegating. I will e-mail you an eight-step process. You look it over, try it out, and next time we talk let me know what you think."

The Eight-Step Process of Delegation

1. What does the desired outcome look like?

2. When do you need it by?

3. What's the budget?

4. What resources do they get?

5. What decisions can they make?

6. What decisions do they need to check with you on?

7. Do you want checkpoints along the way? (You should have specific dates you will meet and evaluate progress and answer questions.)

8. How will we both know and measure how well the task is done? (Be specific.)

I sent him these eight steps and I learned in a subsequent conversation he was using them and he told me how effective they were. He said he didn't use them for simpler projects, but in more complicated situations he forced himself to slow down and use the eight steps. That was when they were most needed. He found results came faster and he didn't have to ask others to redo their work.

Communicating with the Boss

I shifted the conversation by asking a general question to see if he was experiencing any friction or uneasiness with anyone he worked with.

There was no pause. "Yes, my boss. I go into his office to debrief a project he assigned me and we argue. He tells me my results are not what he had in mind. I correct him and make it clear my results are exactly what he asked for.

"He pushes back. I push back. The conversation deteriorates.

"I leave talking to myself. My team and I worked hard to give him what he wants and to fit his projects in with our normal workload. He has miscommunicated his expectations before and he'll do it again. My only consolation is that no boss lasts forever."

Steady There Before You React

I took a deep breath hoping Tom would do the same. "Can you set your frustration aside and let me ask a question?"

He nodded and I said, "You know the delegation process works when you manage down. Would it work to manage up?"

After a very long pause, he started laughing. "Is this another time you will quote the comic book character Pogo: 'We have met the enemy and I am him?'"

I said, "You are the problem and not your boss. It's your responsibility to manage up and to help your boss be successful."

The simplicity of it became obvious to Tom. "I use the delegation process for my team but it never crossed my mind that I should use it with my boss. This is obvious now that I think about it. This could significantly change our conversations and my relationship with my boss. Going forward I commit to using the process. I can see how a frustration can be resolved and I'm hopeful."

It Gets Better

The light bulb brightened. "In the past when we talked, I was locked into the mindset that we had put a lot of work into giving him what we thought he wanted, so I tried to convince him that what he wanted was what we gave him. He's probably been thinking I don't listen to him because this was not what he asked for."

"Tom, a universal blind spot, one common to all of us, is we don't stop to ask ourselves, 'What part of the problems am I?'" I offered. "You now see yours, you own it, and you will change. Remember this, because you were blaming your boss and hoping for a new one."

TOM'S TAKEAWAYS:

- I uncovered my blind spot and it was a breakthrough.

- My boss was a problem, but I was the bigger problem.

- Going forward I'll ask, "What part of the problem do I cause?"

I Want Respect

"Peter is a peer of mine," said Lydia. "He's in sales; I'm customer support and a subject-matter expert. When our customers come to town for a meeting he doesn't introduce me, and he dominates the meeting."

Lydia went on to say he was disrespectful and arrogant. She had met with him and spelled out the specific behaviors that bothered her and were demeaning.

"He told me I was too sensitive and to get over it." She mouthed each word slowly. "I don't want to be seen as overly aggressive; however, it's obvious I need to be blunt."

I'd learned that Lydia will go along until her values are challenged. Now her objective was to get the respect and collaboration she deserved.

At the beginning, we strategized on her next steps but we couldn't get much traction. Then I read to her the definition of partnership from the Center for Creative Leadership. "Partnership: A relationship in which we are jointly committed to the success of whatever we engage in."

Lydia got excited when she heard this. "That definition is just what we need. I will schedule a meeting and start with this definition. Hopefully, the meeting will lead to a productive conversation and an acknowledgment that we are partners."

She had the meeting and reported back, "The guy's a jerk."

Peter had told her, "I am sales and produce revenue; you are support and are an expense. We are in no way partners."

Be Prepared to Lean into the Conversation

Lydia countered. "Peter, what do you think our boss's reaction would be if I quoted to him what you just said about sales and customer support not being partners?"

He shrugged this off. Lydia knew he wanted to be promoted, so she asked, "Do you still want that promotion?" This got his attention. She pressed on. "We both know that collaboration is a cornerstone value for the company. You are not cooperating and if management knew how you were acting you won't get promoted."

Tell Them What You Think of Their Performance

She knew she had the advantage, so she played her cards. "You and I know that before you would ever be promoted, someone would interview those of us you've interacted with to determine if you are promotable. When I'm interviewed, I'll simply give them the facts.

"For instance, when customers come to town, you don't introduce me. You interrupt when I'm answering questions, or you are texting. I'll tell them that out of the fifteen client prep meetings we've scheduled over the past month, you've canceled or changed the times without notifying me thirteen times.

"Then I'll give them the definition of partnership I shared with you and tell them you said we were not partners."

His response was as she expected. "The guy's a chameleon. Once I confronted him he started backpedaling and making excuses."

I Want Respect

Lydia told him, "Peter, you know where I stand. Words won't influence me. Actions will. When you treat me and others with respect and recognize our value, my opinion of you will change."

Lydia went on, "I didn't have to share my thoughts with you, Peter. I could have chosen to not be direct. I made the effort to alert you to give you a second chance. I'm treating you the way I'd like to be treated."

We Want a Second Chance, and So Do They

Peter is human. He is married with three kids and is a hard worker. He likely would eventually have been fired. Even if he didn't get fired, he would never have received the promotion he wanted. If we care about our coworkers, if we are truly partners, and we see they are going to act their way out of a job or further advancement, we have to speak up. By having the conversation, Lydia gave Peter a second chance.

LYDIA'S TAKEAWAYS:

- First care about them, then tell the impact they are having on you.

- You won't be heard if you don't speak up. It's risky at times, but the reward can be significant.

- Speaking up is a skill you can develop. Read some of the other stories and learn how.

Influencers Ask Good Questions

These are not just stories helping my clients see what they can do and where their blind spots are. I have had my own growth opportunities. My story starts at home, but I know you will see the application at work as well.

Why Waste My Time?

One Friday my wife got a call from our neighbor with an invite to dinner Saturday. I didn't want to go. It would be nice people replaying old tapes, much like going to a meeting at work because you are expected to show up.

When I heard the invite, my self-talk was, "I can guess what everyone will say at dinner—why bother going? This is a waste of my time."

I was in clenched-jaw mode when something annoying happened.

A faint inner voice said, "How can you make a difference?" I was irked by the question and busied myself with other activities; however, the sense I should do something about my attitude would not go away.

My complaint was that the group's conversations covered familiar ground. What could I do to change this? I liked that this question was moving me out of being a victim into being a solution. I prefer to be a spectator at events like this, but I had to recognize I was passive and part of the problem.

My goal was clear—change the conversation from boring to interesting. But how would I do this? I'd read that "significant conversations had a significant question embedded in them."

The Value of a Good Question

First, the question had to be in context. Then I had to consider the components of a good question. It needed to be brief, direct, thought-provoking, and needed to touch their experience. My question was, "What is one of the riskiest things you've ever done? It can be physical, financial, or emotional."

Doing the Right Thing May Feel Wrong

On our way to the party, I told my wife what I had in mind and she was lukewarm. I started to think maybe she was right, that I shouldn't say anything. Maybe it would be better to keep quiet and once again just get through the evening enduring the same tired conversation topics.

The eight of us were comfortably seated at the neighbor's dining room table. Dinner was finished and there was a pause before dessert. A nervous me told myself to not rush the question, but first, tell why I was asking the question.

Tell Them Your Intent or the Why

"As neighbors, we get together occasionally but we don't know much about each other," I began. "I went to a funeral of an acquaintance and learned things I'd never heard. He won a citywide spelling bee, was last in his college graduating class but among the first to sail from California to Hawaii.

"I have a question I'd like each of us to answer so we can learn more about each other. I suggest someone volunteer to go first. We'll listen, ask a few questions, be sensitive to time as others follow, and we'll go around the table."

One of the men groaned and mumbled something negative about dumb games. I was uncomfortable, wishing I would have suffered in silence as I had before.

The hostess came to the rescue. "What is your question?"

The Question

My answer was, "What is one of the riskiest things you've ever done? It can be physical, financial, or emotional."

Our hostess didn't hesitate. "I'm from a small Midwest town, the only daughter of a successful father. As a single mom, I didn't want to hang around town any longer. I headed west with my three-month-old son. I did bookkeeping work, and used this experience to start a financial services business."

With ease people connected with her answer and offered an encouraging comment. The ice was broken and hands were raised to go next. The conversation got animated, and there was not the customary mass exodus after dessert.

I heard a lot of, "I didn't know that about you," followed by, "We have several things in common." Conversations flowed for the rest of the evening because there were common interests.

Build an Inventory of Good Questions

Work on building an inventory of good questions. Questions are powerful. Have you noticed individuals progressing in organizations shift from giving answers to asking questions? They let go of their egos to challenge others to grow. To let go is to stop controlling others. It is a vote of confidence that leads to trust, which in turn builds a strong team.

TAKEAWAYS:

- Being a bump on a log is safer, but not nearly as satisfying as participating.

- If you want to be an influencer, ask good questions.

- Good questions can build confidence within groups.

6

Turn Your Frustration with a Job into a Better Job

....

The way you look at circumstances can turn frustration with your current job into a better job or stress into quiet assurance. You may not be able to change your work circumstances, but you can change how you react. Listen to a coaching session with Ernest.

Ernest could put anyone at ease and was usually upbeat, but today he was discouraged. He was worn down by circumstances—namely, the turnover in his department.

It was not normal turnover. The turnover was caused by other managers in the company pilfering his most productive employees. Just as they became productive, along came offers to move upward and onward. You couldn't blame them for taking a better offer, but the impact was Ernest couldn't meet deadlines and fell behind on his deliverables. His performance reviews were below average.

Take Advantage of Unfavorable Circumstances

"Ernest, how can you take advantage of these circumstances? That is, find a way to manage the turnover to your advantage," I asked.

"Are you playing mind games with me or is that a serious question?" Ernest replied.

My response was, "It's a serious question. You can't change the circumstances. Your boss doesn't have your back. Managers see you as a training ground and they like that you save them time training and locating talent."

Ernest gave me a blank look and I went on. "You're spending your energy being defensive, and you can't win. Stop defending what you have and change the way you react."

I repeated my question, "How can you manage turnover to your advantage? Start with the positive. What are the positives?"

Forget Your Job Description and Think about the Results You Get

"I like to train people and help their careers," said Ernest. "If I didn't lose them it would be great. It's more energizing than what I currently do, which is to deal with boring data and projects."

I Found a Better Job and I Didn't Have to Leave the Company to Find It

I could hardly contain myself, "What if you turned your thinking upside-down and stopped getting frustrated because they leave and started seeing yourself as the internal training department to help people advance in their careers? I would think your company would applaud that."

Recharged, but ever practical, Ernest pointed out his boss was never around and was the most narcissistic man he knew. Once again, the challenge was to change from bemoaning he had a difficult boss to focus on the desired outcome.

Focus on the Desired Outcome

"Ernest, I have a question. What do you have to do to influence your boss?"

Ernest said, "I have to ask myself this question: 'How can I change the way I normally react to my boss (which is to roll my eyes) into something that would make him look good and appeal to his narcissistic nature?'

"My answer is, I can give him the general vision, then point out that when it's implemented others will applaud his strategic thinking in seeing how an internal employee development center increased morale, built bench strength and saved on search costs."

There were bumps in the road, but Ernest saw how he could create his ideal job, so he excelled at overcoming objections.

ERNEST'S TAKEAWAYS:

• Carving out a niche where you work is better than looking for another job.

• You can turn your frustration and talent into a better job if you think creatively.

• Everyone is suited for the right job. It's a matter of leaning in and looking for opportunities.

Help Your Managers Know What They Want

••

Donna met me at the receptionist's desk. She was rubbing her neck as we walked down the hall. She was obviously stressed.

My Manager Knows How to Frustrate Me

We went to an office for our coaching session. As the door closed, she said, "Ed is a manager whose goal is to frustrate me. I know you—you will suggest I talk to him, but it's hard.

Her moist eyes were on me.

I began with, "You probably feel there is nothing you can say to Ed. There may be a way you can get more comfortable telling him how he is impacting your performance.

"Let's do this: give me some background information on why you're working here and your relationship with Ed. Then we'll see if we can find a solution for your frustration."

Donna told me she'd been in the same company with Ed in Chicago. There was a merger and they both lost their jobs. Her next company folded, so she called Ed to network and happened to mention how much she had learned about software since they last spoke.

They Hired You Because They Need You

Ed started asking rapid-fire questions, drilling deeper each time. After twenty minutes he offered Donna a job. She explained her current situation with the kids in school, the negative house value, and poor timing. Ed responded that he would pay all moving expenses, including the mortgage shortfall, and offered a salary increase of 20 percent.

"I needed a job so I moved," said Donna. "They asked me to review their pick for a company to do a major software upgrade. They'd picked a poor company. I almost used them until I did exhaustive due diligence and found they didn't deliver on commitments."

Look at the Value You Add

"Ed got lucky finding you at just the right time," I said. "I doubt you know your value."

Suppressing my hope that she'd saved them a bundle, I calmly asked, "Do you have any way of knowing how much money you've saved the company?"

I asked several questions, scribbling down numbers along the way. By my calculations, she'd recovered not only the moving expenses, but the software improvements had also saved the company the equivalent of her first year's salary.

We continued down the path of establishing her value. "If Ed fired you or you quit, what do you think it would cost the company?"

She had no idea, so I related an *Inc.* magazine article that listed these costs: lower productivity due to the loss of the person who left and the time to find a replacement, overworked remaining staff, lost knowledge, training costs, interviewing costs, and recruiters' fees. Overall, estimated costs can add up to as high as 150 percent of an employee's annual salary.

"Donna, by now you should see yourself differently. Reset your thinking. You are a valuable asset."

A Difficult Conversation Made Doable

"You told yourself a story: 'Ed's goal is to frustrate me.' You don't know that! Lose your made-up story."

I continued. "Before you talk to him, check yourself to see if you are in the right frame of mind. Can you see him as a fellow flawed human being? If you aren't in a judgmental state of mind, you are ready."

Donna interrupted, "Do you have any idea how hard it is to give anyone feedback, particularly my manager? The status quo may not be ideal, but I can cope."

"Before you limit yourself," I said, "let me walk you through a way to give Ed feedback. Then you decide whether to talk to him or not.

"You've told me your boss gives you complex projects with little direction. The problem is he doesn't know how to delegate. If he had a process, something like a delegation checklist, you both would have a roadmap."

Give Your Manager a Tool That Helps

Donna was listening, so I continued. "Pick a time when he isn't rushed. Go to a quiet place, and put him at ease by saying, 'Ed, I get lost on projects you give me. I don't have a roadmap. I should have said something long ago. I can bring it up now because I just figured out my problem and the solution. It's a simple eight-item checklist. Here is a copy. It's a roadmap to get from point *A* to point *B*.'"

This is the checklist I offered, with clarifying comments after each question.

1. What does the outcome look like? The answer provides both qualitative and quantitative data.

2. When do you need it by? This may be an end date or periodic milestones.

3. What's the budget? This may apply or may not.

4. What resources do I get? People or money?

5. What decisions can I make? Ed will be interrupted less.

6. What decisions do I need to check with you on? Managers like to be in control.

7. When will we schedule checkpoints along the way? This keeps you on target.

8. How will we both know and measure how well the task is done? Be specific.

Donna liked the checklist because it was tangible. She could give it to him, write down his answers, and ask questions for clarification along the way.

Feeling Good, I'm Dealing Better with My Manager

At our next meeting, she was relaxed and smiling.

"The hard conversation was worth it," said Donna. "It's the first time I've had clarity on what he wanted. I think it's the first time he's had clarity on what he wanted. You'll love this. A few days ago he started to dump a project on me as he headed out the door. I said, 'I can't start on this project until we sit down and go through the eight-step delegation checklist.'"

DONNA'S TAKEAWAYS:

- Helping your manager know what he wants is a win-win.

- Giving a boss feedback can be one of the hardest things we do at work, but it's also one of the most rewarding.

- If you can follow these principles and have that feedback conversation with your boss, it will be one of the most powerful levers you have to fix your frustrations at work.

COACH'S COMMENT:

Conflict is part of life. Don't be surprised when it comes up. It can surface issues that need to be dealt with, and this is a good thing.

Knowledge is of no value unless you put it into practice.
— Anton Chekov

▶ Important Feedback Checklist

- Colleagues will frustrate you. If it's a minor issue, let it go. If it builds, address it.

- No one can read your mind, so if you don't explain the problem, you are the problem.

- Check your attitude and frame of mind before you talk to someone. If you don't care for him or her as a person, it's a deeper issue.

- If the conversation is about something that happened:

    - Refresh the person's memory on the situation.

    - Be specific in a nonjudgmental manner, describing the behavior and how you want the behavior changed.

    - Express the impact it had on you, including the emotional content.

Family Lessons in Leadership

David was an oncologist. He worked for a large pharmaceutical company that was heavily invested in developing a drug for a specific type of cancer.

I knew David in a social setting, where I had also met his three accomplished adult children. One day, with a shy smile, he lowered his voice and told me his boss wanted him to find a coach and get leadership training. He asked if I was interested. I was, and I suggested David introduce me to his supervisor, Mike, so I could get his perspective.

The Problem

"David is a world-class oncologist," said Mike. "However, he is spending 80 percent of his time being a scientist and only 20 percent leading his team of doctors."

"Have you told David this?" I asked.

"I think I've told him this. I wish he spent 80 percent of his time leading his team. The team's goal is to prepare new drug applications for submission to the Food and Drug Administration," said Mike.

Owning the Feedback

After I talked to Mike, David and I met in his office. He closed the door, sat at his desk, and leaned forward on his elbows. "So, what did you learn?"

After I told him exactly what Mike had told me, David's eyes grew big. He rose slowly to his feet. I had no idea how he was going to react. Would he be upset because Mike hadn't been clear on expectations and blame Mike?

"He is right; I have not been doing my job, based on what you just told me," David said. "Mike may have told me this before, or not, but the point is now I know."

David was a very rare bird, and I told him so. "Some would fly off the handle with this news. Others would squawk. You, however, own it," I said. "You skipped the time-consuming blaming of your boss or the denial stage. Congratulations. Now we can go straight to developing you as a leader."

It may be normal to become defensive, but you won't grow this way.

And that's what we did. Over the next four months, I benchmarked David's leadership skills through interviews and by shadowing him. He didn't get defensive when I gave him feedback, yet there was a dose of scientific skepticism. One time David mentioned he thought I was spending too much time interviewing his team and observing him. I took great delight in saying, "David, I would be guilty of malpractice if I didn't do a thorough diagnosis."

We talked about how to resolve conflict, how to create a safe environment to foster creativity, and how to develop relationships. Yet I knew David did not completely understand. Even though he was listening to me and growing, David did not see himself as a leader, nor did he understand the difference a leader could make.

Late on a Friday afternoon, we sat in David's office. A thought pressed in on me. I said, "David, your three children are extremely accomplished. What is your secret?"

This was obviously a topic he was passionate about. He launched into an animated explanation.

"Raising the kids was relatively easy until they got into their teens and beyond," he said. "Now I had to guide them without guiding them, to listen without fixing, and, when necessary, tell them things they didn't want to hear. I had to stop issuing orders and think through what I was going to say, how to say it, and when to say it."

David was on a roll. "They would get anxious about difficult situations and wanted me to tell them what to do. I resisted because I knew they would never grow up or develop their own character if they didn't have to wrestle with the situation. I started asking them a lot of questions and saying very little. I let them make mistakes. This was painful to watch. I was proactive in building guardrails around my emotions as best I could."

Eureka, He Gets It

When he stopped I just sat there for a moment. Then I asked him if he saw a parallel between what he just said about raising his children and what we'd been talking about for the last four months.

He looked perplexed and paused, but not for very long. As the realization hit him he started laughing so loudly I had to shut the door.

"My children are proof I have people skills," said David. "I don't have to learn them—I have them. All I need to do is treat my docs as I treated my children. This will be my inner secret and I'll smile every time I think of it."

Applying the Lessons

As a coach, I am reminded of the adage, "You cannot teach anybody anything. You can only make them think." The first lesson is that David discovered that he had basic leadership skills and learned how to apply them to guiding his brilliant doctors.

Another lesson from this story falls on the shoulders of Mike. Why had he never clearly explained his expectations? David, to his credit, didn't get defensive; he heard the message, committed to change, and led the team to a successful outcome.

A third lesson is that sometimes progress takes time. Some might ask why it took four months for David to get it. Well, I'd like to jump out of bed and go run a marathon. But the reality is, I'm not in shape and I'd need to train for it. David and I agreed he'd be in training for four months. The military spends mega dollars on training, believing that "You fight the way you train." We lead and react the way we train.

This story has a happy ending. Thanks to David's leadership, the company's submission to the Food & Drug Administration was accepted.

DAVID'S TAKEAWAYS:

- I applied my skill at teaching family lessons to being a better leader at work.

- Feedback provides a choice. I chose to use it to grow.

I Almost Quit, but Now I'm Fine

I sent Linda a biography to complete before we had our first coaching session. One question was, "Deep down inside of you, what is your concern?"

Her Concern Was, "I'll Be a Bag Lady."

Linda wore an expression of wariness as she sat forward in her chair. She was a highly introverted mid-level manager.

"Tell me about the situation with your boss," I began.

"He is causing me major stress and anxiety. I spend hours preparing for our Monday team meetings. I script what I want to say. I barely get into my script and he interrupts with a question."

She rushed on. "It's disruptive and puts me on my back foot. It totally takes me out of my script. I feel lost and foolish. I can't focus on both my script and his question. I wish I were quicker on my feet. Others are—I'm not."

When she paused, I asked if she'd talked to her boss about his interrupting her. She said she had not—that she didn't handle conflict well.

I tried a different perspective. "Linda, if your boss stepped on your foot and it hurt, what would you do?"

"I'd say ouch," she replied, "but if I said anything to him about interrupting he'd probably tell me to get over it, answer his questions, and move on."

Would You Tell a Friend She's Frustrating You?

How about outside of work? When one of your close friends frustrates you and you can't avoid the situation any longer, how do you tell your friend that you're frustrated?" I asked.

Long pause. "I'd tell my friend what she did that frustrated me, and if it continues what it would do to our friendship. I would be honest, open, and vulnerable."

"Can you do the same thing with your boss?" I asked.

"I'm the only woman on the leadership team," she responded. "If I go down the honest, open, vulnerability path, I risk losing credibility and my ability to influence."

"Linda, I know the fear you have of losing your job," I said. "Before our next meeting, make a list of pros and a list of cons for your job, talk to friends, and we'll discuss what you want to do."

At our next meeting, there was no pros/cons list. Linda said, "My boss's behavior is causing me so much stress I'm ready to quit. I have nothing to lose now, so let's go back to the points you made earlier about having a difficult conversation. I will be vulnerable by telling him the emotional impact his interruptions have on me."

Have You Judged Him?

"Linda, before you have this conversation," I said with conviction, "or any other meaningful one, please check your mindset. Have you judged, tried, and convicted him of being a bad boss, or can you move to a more caring and neutral frame of mind?

"Think of him as human—flawed, but trying to be the best he can. Just as you'd like a second chance, give him one."

Linda agreed and we role played the following scenario: "Boss, I am frustrated and I'm the problem because I haven't told you what is frustrating me. I'm an introvert.

"I prepare what I'm going to say for our Monday morning team meetings. I script out what I want to say. But I start by following my script and you interrupt with questions. This breaks the rhythm of my script. I lose my place and get frustrated.

"My fear is I will say something foolish. I'm starting to stutter. I've never stuttered in my life. I'm not sleeping well. I tell myself to get over it and it shouldn't bother me. It doesn't work and that makes me feel worse.

"There is a solution. If you would, please hold your questions, let me finish, then look over at me and ask, 'Linda are you finished?' Do this and I won't be stressed. I won't fear Monday team meetings and I will be a more relaxed, productive me."

After we role-played, Linda had the conversation and the boss changed. More significant was the change in Linda. She saw how she could influence her boss and others and was more confident because she faced the fear of speaking up.

LINDA'S TAKEAWAYS:

- I almost quit, but now I'm fine.

- I'll tell my friends to never quit without trying to improve the situation first.

- I faced my fear and now I'm stronger.

- Ask yourself on a regular basis:

- Is there a conversation I'm avoiding?

- How is my silence affecting me and others?

- If the roles were reversed, would I want them to talk to me?

10

How to Survive Mergers and Downsizings

....

Judy explained three ways she miraculously survived four layoffs:

1. I learned to actively seek the welfare of others.

2. It was riskier to not tell the boss what's really going on.

3. I stopped blaming the dysfunctional workplace and asked myself how I could be high functioning.

1. Actively Seek the Welfare of Others

"During a performance review, my tight-lipped boss referenced too many people stopping by my desk to talk. I started paying attention to what we talked about, which was answering questions about where to find things, who to talk to about a problem, or giving a word of encouragement.

"I told this to my boss, but he didn't see the cumulative value of these conversations. Since he is visual, I put a large glass jar on my desk and asked for a penny for answers to questions or help-giving. I had two inches of pennies in a short time and the boss asked about it, which of course was the reason for the jar. I told him each penny was a conversation and gave him examples of how I had listened to others, connected them with the right people, and shared how I'd resolved problems. I was free to give him examples because he had asked. I had told him what the conversations were about before, but he's the kind of person who doesn't listen until he asks the question.

"I don't know if my boss got it, but I do know by this time I had so much social capital that I felt I'd be one of the last to go. There is an additional benefit—I'd have so many friends who were let go before me and found other jobs, and they'd get me an interview at their new company."

You may not have a jar of pennies, but you can also build relationships and emotional capital. Love is a hard word to define, but try this definition: "to actively seek the welfare of others." Pause and think about this. Don't you seek the welfare of your family members and friends, sometimes even sacrificing your own interests? *Could you also apply this at work? If you can, you'll reap rewards both material and emotional.*

2. Tell the Boss What's Really Going On

Judy told me of an idea the boss had implemented that backfired and had the opposite impact he intended.

My reaction was to share what I'd experienced. I told her, "When I ask bosses about their teams, they start by telling me what each person does. Then the bosses highlight one or two employees whom they value, who will take a risk by giving them feedback on their weaknesses as a boss and are even quick to point out dumb ideas."

Judy asked for an example of how to give bosses feedback in a way that doesn't upset them. Here it is.

Assume your boss asks you, "What can I do to improve my effectiveness?" You say something like, "If you would slow down when delegating, I could ask clarifying questions and get you better results."

Bosses are interested in results, so you're speaking their language. You made a minor request, but when your boss sees better results, the payoff is major.

More examples of minor requests you can make of bosses and peers that will yield major payoffs:

- If I know the "why" behind the request, I feel informed, included, and trusted. That's motivating.

- If you're smiling and relaxed, we are too.

- If you had a chart that shows how everyone's contribution relates, that would paint the bigger picture.

In these scenarios, the boss is being tested with minor suggestions to see if action would be taken.

If you are worried that speaking up will make you look bad, listen to what actually went on behind closed doors in one company I worked with while deciding which of two employees to lay off. The leader of the panel said, "Susie keeps her head down and works hard. Jason works hard, is a pain at times, but makes good suggestions. Let's keep Jason."

3. In a Dysfunctional Workplace, You Can Be High-Functioning

Outstanding collaborators survive when superstars burn out. The superstar is focused on self to the exclusion of others. Collaborators actively seek the welfare of others, the people they work with, as well as customers. As a result, they are valued.

What might valuing others look like? Say you're having coffee with a few coworkers when one mentions how Margaret seems aloof. You resist the temptation to agree. Instead, you say, "I thought something similar until I made an effort to get to know her. Now I feel differently."

It may be that you are struggling with a relationship with your boss or a coworker. Even when it's difficult, commit yourself to making that person look good. It's not easy to do, but just grind your teeth and do it. The alternative is to hope it will get better. It probably won't. Take the high ground. It will pay dividends since this attitude removes competition, opening the door for you to be heard and valued.

TAKEAWAYS:

- You can stand out and be viewed as a collaborator by actively seeking the welfare of others.

- Tell your bosses how their decisions impact others.

- Take the high ground. Build up others, don't take the low road and gossip.

11

Small Talk Is Big Talk

∙∙

Listen to yourself—you may already have the answers.

Donovan, a coaching client, was smiling while scratching his head. "Are you serious? You're telling me, based on what I told you, that if I will listen to myself, I can relate better to people, which will lead to a promotion?"

My response was, "Let me quote back to you what you said earlier in our conversation: 'I'm uncomfortable with the idea of mixing business with my personal life. Business and personal should be separate. That's what I've been told, but that's not what I see happening around me. I'm in the entertainment business and people seem to know a lot about each other. These guys are talking about vacations, what they did over the weekend, and about things they have in common. There is often lots of laughter.'"

After a pause, I asked: "Are you able to make small talk and share more of yourself in the same way?"

Share Enough about Yourself

"Not really. The model I learned early on was to keep it on a professional business level. But I do try—I ask my coworkers a lot of questions."

I asked, "Do you know more about them than they know about you?" Donovan's smile disappeared. "I'm not comfortable talking about myself, so we don't find common ground. There is no exchange, so conversations don't last long."

"I hope you are listening to yourself," I said. "You just identified your stumbling block to relationships."

We Live in a Two-Way-Street World

Donovan's smile returned, "Wow, I see it now! I live on a one-way street."

I pressed on. "Do you understand that to change your behavior you need to be highly motivated, recognize relationships will be messy, and be prepared for hard work?"

His response was immediate. "Relationships, that is, who you know in the entertainment business, are vital. My boss isn't that swift, but he knows a lot of people and they take his phone calls. That's why he has a job. That's why he's been promoted. I want to be promoted. I am highly motivated."

Donovan's mood changed to a man with a mission. "I get it. I haven't invested in relationships. Do you have any suggestions?"

Building Relationships

"I can share what I've seen work," I began. "Relationship builders start with a mindset of curiosity and interest in others. They make small talk and ask questions in a gentle way to get to know the person.

"A block to openness is judging a person based on what you've heard. Instead of a preconceived idea, put aside rumors and gossip and approach others expecting the best.

"Relationship builders check their motives. We can quickly discern the givers from the takers. Givers are supporters who find ways to help those around them."

Donovan was ready for implementation. "You said, 'Relationship builders ask questions in a gentle way to get to know the person.' Where do I get the questions?"

"My favorite book on questions is *The Complete Book of Questions: 1001 Conversation Starters for any Occasion*, by Garry Poole," I replied. "Good questions invite people to open up, and are a safe way to initiate conversations. In their answers, you'll find the common ground you mentioned earlier and a way of continuing conversations. Start by practicing with people around you."

Frame the Question—Don't Just Jump In

"You may feel awkward asking questions. Ease into it by telling them why you are asking the question—something like, 'We've never really talked—would you tell me about the job you had before this one and a little about your family if that's all right?'"

Donovan was receptive, so I kept going. "After you know the person a little better and if you're hoping for a deeper relationship, you have to be vulnerable. You will have to go first. Something like, 'I'm struggling with an issue at work and would welcome your feedback.'"

Donovan jumped in. "What you described is a two-way street. I get it."

DONOVAN'S TAKEAWAYS:

- Small talk is big talk when it comes to building relationships and moving forward in your career.

- You want a balanced relationship where colleagues know as much about you as you do about them. Good questions build good relationships.

Your Decisions Affect Others—Look Deeply

"When you're working with refugee detention camps, you need the whole picture."

This is how Mary started our coaching session. I had coached her for a year when she was VP of a private company before she took her current government job. I had never heard this level of tension in her voice.

She said, "I need to slow down and give you some background information." Taking a deep breath, she continued. "Our immigration department, like yours in the United States, is short-handed, so we use outside attorneys.

"As the newly appointed head of my government's legal team, I saw an opportunity to save six million dollars by not outsourcing the contracts we use with the refugee detention center for purveyors of food, bedding, and education.

"My expertise in contracts was one of the reasons I was hired, but I soon found my team had no experience. I had to spend hours training them, in small groups and one-on-one meetings. Although I begrudged the time away from my family, my husband understood that I had to build a stronger team and to prove they'd made a good decision when they hired me.

"I don't want to work that hard again for a long, long time. The good news was they gained respect for my professional skills and I have a stronger team. In the future, I can spend more time with my family. My boss was amazed since the legal department had never undertaken such a complex task. They'd always outsourced. My boss's boss was pleased, too."

Your Decisions Affect Others

I was curious. "Sounds like you stepped up and performed, so why are you upset?"

She explained, "The contracts we wrote are well-crafted, giving the government protection they haven't had in the past. We gave the outside suppliers very little wiggle room. But there's another perspective.

"Contracts impact people. They are not just business transactions. I didn't get the people impact until I made my first visit to the detention camp. I talked to the refugees, the suppliers, and the guards about the quality of life and services.

"The guards thought things were fine and best left alone. The refugees, though, had legitimate complaints. The suppliers said most of those complaints could be taken care of with the same amount of money we'd contracted for, but the terms of the contracts didn't allow the flexibility to meet the needs. The suppliers' hands were tied. As I walked around I was so struck by the poor conditions I had to hide my tears behind my sunglasses.

"I was upset with me. I should have visited the camps before we wrote the contracts. It's dumb to think you can sit behind a desk and make good decisions. Fortunately, I can tweak the existing contracts to better serve the refugees at no additional cost."

MARY'S TAKEAWAYS:

- Talk to the people affected by a decision before you make the decision.

- Decisions made just on facts or data without the whole picture may lead to poor decisions.

Get Their Help with a Smile

How can you ask for help and make it fun? Sit back and relax. Let me have some fun telling you a story, and when you reach the end, you'll get an idea of how to get help with a smile.

My wife, Jill, and I have been going to the same restaurant every Saturday morning for years. Only recently, though, have I figured out how to order breakfast.

What puzzled me is that I've been giving what I considered straightforward breakfast orders for years. Often, what I receive is not at all what I expected. Other times it's close, but not close enough to kick off a good Saturday morning.

On a recent Saturday, we entered our spot. Shortly after we were seated the waitress came to the table. She recognized us and after the usual pleasantries, she asked if we were ready to order.

I commenced with my usual recitation: "I would like two eggs over medium, bacon crispy, hash browns crispy, and no toast; instead, grilled tomatoes, and I like my food hot."

I Didn't Get What I Wanted

Soon the meal arrived. The eggs were too runny to be called over medium; the hash browns were limp and light brown; the bacon wasn't crispy. At all. It had those little fatty bubbles on each side. The tomatoes were not grilled, and the food was not hot.

How Do You Get What You Want and Keep the Harmony?

What can I do, I thought to myself, *to manage a better outcome and still keep the peace with Jill?*

Jill likes harmony. She likes the restaurant. She likes our Saturday morning breakfasts. So, I wasn't sure what to do. Should I complain and set a tone that is uncomfortable for Jill or do I let it slide? I decided to let it slide, but then I was upset with myself at how I was dealing with the problem. I felt silent and passive. Then I rationalized to myself, *No, it's no big deal. Jill's peace of mind is more important.*

The waitress returned to the table, holding a pot of hot coffee in one hand and a pitcher of ice water in the other.

"How was your food?" she asked indifferently.

"Fine," I said. "Could I please have the check?" I left a less than average tip.

Ask the Right Question and You're Half Way to the Right Answer

The following Saturday I was determined that ordering breakfast would be different. My thought centered on a key question: *How can I make the waitress smile and also get the exact breakfast I want?*

This time, it was a different waitress. "Are you ready to order?"

I took a deep breath and looked up at her with a warm smile.

"Yes, I know exactly what I want for breakfast. I hope you won't think I'm an overly demanding jerk, but I want you to know exactly what I want so when I finish my breakfast I'll be happy and you'll be happy with my tip."

My smile broadened and I continued, "I know serving people is a tough job. Actually, I have a confession that I want to make to you. I'm an HFF. Don't worry, it's not contagious—I'm a Hot Food Fanatic. For me, hot food is good food. Serving food on a hot plate makes a difference and I know a hot plate isn't easy to handle. Can you do that?"

She nodded yes.

"Great, here is what I want. I want the egg whites firm, and the yolks–I don't want them runny and I don't want them hard. I would like to have them medium. The hash browns, I would like cooked to a golden brown and crunchy. The bacon crispy. I don't want toast. Instead, I would like grilled tomatoes. Grilled tomatoes remind me of when I was a kid in the Midwest."

Trust Your Instincts

At this point, Jill was rolling her eyes. I looked at her and thought that eye-rolling was a good trade-off if I got the breakfast I wanted. The internal problem was for me to remain silent and let the hoped-for results speak for themselves. I shifted in my seat.

The order came and it was perfect. I let the waitress know. "This breakfast is just what I wanted," I said with an even bigger smile than before. "If there is a waitress of the month, you've got my vote! I know you shift table assignments each week, but next Saturday we'll ask for you."

TAKEAWAYS:

How can you ask for their help and make it fun?

- Be relaxed, be creative.

- Let them know the reason for your request.

- Tell them the difference their help will make.

- Be specific, using your creativity, and if it's appropriate feel free to use a little exaggeration.

14

The Pitfall of "It's All About Me"

··

As we settled in to discuss the probability of a promotion for Carl, I asked, "What's your worldview on people?"

What You Think about Others Is How You'll Treat Them

"I'm skeptical about people," he said. "I find they are stupid and slow to get things." I asked how that was working for him.

Carl, a mid-thirties, street-smart, cocky sales manager, looked me in the eye and said, "It's working. But I do treat my team differently." He spoke with confidence, "I jump on them but they know I have their back. I protect them, so in my closed circle it works."

"What about outside that closed circle?" I asked.

With no apparent regret, he said, "There are a few customers I connect with, but mostly I just get along. Customers generally aren't too bright so I tolerate them."

What Your Coworkers Think Counts

I was blunt and shared the results of his company assessment. "Based on these comments, your worldview isn't working with your coworkers." I read him an example: "He is self-serving.

His direct nature comes off as harsh or crass when interacting with others."

He stayed in character when he said smugly, "I didn't think I was that easy to read." Then he surprised me. "I am self-centered," he said, "and it has worked...up until now."

I asked what he meant by "up until now."

The Truth about You Can Free You from You

He revealed something deeper. "I aspire to move up the ladder and it's obvious my attitude doesn't position me to lead in this company." In a slightly softened tone, he said, "I've got to change." I asked him how he might go about changing.

"I'll start by changing my view of people," he said. I then asked the obvious question: "How do you do that?"

Slightly chastened, Carl said, "I don't know and I would welcome some thoughts or suggestions."

I wanted to ask Carl how long it had been since he'd given someone permission to give him advice, but I didn't for fear of derailing the coaching session.

I told him that, if his mind was set on promotion, he would figure out how to change in time. Then I added, "Some people who are self-absorbed are humbled by the immensity of the universe. They marvel at creation and the creator."

Carl thought for a moment and said, "I don't connect with that point of view; nevertheless, I do need to take change more seriously and do something. I guess I'll fake it until I make it."

What Does "A Control Freak in Recovery" Mean?

He changed the subject, "Earlier in our conversation, we talked about my need to be in control and you started laughing because you said you were a lot like me, but now you were a control freak in recovery. What did you mean by that?"

I told him I was hesitant to answer because God is involved and God talk isn't in. I was smiling. Carl smiled back and said, "Give me the short version and don't preach!" We both laughed.

I began. "I bootstrapped a business to success over fourteen years. The success was fatal because it attracted stiff competition. I closed the business. What shocked me was that my business was my identity. I felt that I was a glass of water poured out on the sand. The glass was empty. I no longer existed.

"That is when the panic attacks started. I was so desperate, I cried out, 'God, if you really exist I need help and I need it now!'

"Do you want me to continue?"

He nodded.

God Asks Me a Tough Question

"This is why I say that I'm a control freak in recovery. Two weeks after my cry for help, I woke at 1:23 a.m. to an unspoken yet clear question: *Who do you want to be in control, you or me?*

"*Silence.* With silence, there is no dialogue. There was just the question hanging in space waiting for an answer. I offered up, 'You know control is what I rely on. Why would I want to relinquish control?' *Silence.*

'You are asking me to let go of who I am.' *Silence.*

"This was the end of my encounter, but this story is still unfolding because my early years were ones of a tight grip. I'm better today, but I'm not where I'd like to be, so I'm a control freak in recovery."

Carl, it's Your Story; You Write the Rest of It

Carl reacted to my story with a question. "You've worked with hundreds of executives. How do you see me five years from now and in the future?"

"If you look beyond self and you focus on helping others and your motive is bigger than just benefiting you, then you will be promoted.

"Your bigger motive involves your purpose in life. You have a purpose, and by diligently seeking, you will find it."

CARL'S TAKEAWAY:

Ask myself the big question: "What is my purpose in life?"

15

Rehearse Difficult Conversations

"I know that Jerry is the boss, but if he publicly flames me once more in an e-mail that has fifteen people copied, I'll quit."

I was on a call with Ella, age twenty-five, who in four months went from worker bee to the supervisor of five people.

I can predict the future. "Jerry will publicly criticize you in an e-mail again, so you're taking a no-win path. Emotions are not reliable guides in life. Take a breath, step back, and look at what you've learned by being in a fast-growing company that promotes from within."

There was a pause, and then I added, "Hopefully you see the logic of cooling down, but a greater concern is your anger. What triggers this anger?"

Identify What Triggers a Negative Reaction, Then Have a Plan to Deal with It

She said, "I interpret his chewing me out in public as a lack of respect." Ella added, "I know I react emotionally and I know the person I harm the most is me, but it's a hair-trigger reaction."

I asked Ella if she had told Jerry what she just told me. She said no, and that the thought had never crossed her mind. She said she was intimidated by Jerry and didn't believe Jerry would listen.

"If Jerry listened to you and didn't correct you in e-mails, do you see a future in the company?"

"Yes."

My response was, "See if this is accurate. If you have a difficult conversation with Jerry and he listens and stops flaming you in e-mails, you'll stay. If you don't have the conversation and Jerry flames you, you'll leave?"

Ella didn't miss a beat. "I'll have the conversation, but I'm not sure of what to say."

"Be genuine and authentic. Tell Jerry exactly what you just told me about the lack of respect and your hair-trigger reaction of anger."

Talent Is Hard to Find

"Jerry knows how hard it is to find and retain young talent," I said. "He must hold you in high regard because he gave you a lot of responsibility. Besides, now is the time to talk to Jerry— you have nothing to lose. You're ready to quit. Be direct with Jerry. This can lead to the respect you crave."

I asked Ella what she thought.

She was ready for the next step. "Like you say, I have more to gain than lose." She rubbed her hands together when she said, "Let's rehearse what I'll say."

Rehearse That Difficult Conversation

This was her rehearsed approach: "Jerry, you know I'm passionate about my work, but what you don't know is that I'm passionate about my work and about being respected.

"I know when you travel you're under pressure to meet with clients and to keep track of what's going on at the office. This is the story I tell myself so I get upset when I receive an e-mail from you chewing me out and see the whole team was copied.

"I need your help in not overreacting to your e-mails. I enjoy my work. You've been good to me—you promoted me. You gave me the opportunities. I believe I have a future here.

"Please understand being disrespected triggers my anger. It's something like an ejection seat in a jet fighter. Please, no more e-mails—pick up the phone and let's talk, or if that isn't possible and you need to chew me out, do it in an e-mail, but don't copy the team."

The conversation took place nine months ago. Jerry heard Ella's respectful request and heeded it. She was promoted and now has direct supervision over twenty employees.

ELLA'S TAKEAWAY:

- You can fix your frustrations at work by facing them.

- Clearly state the facts: what were the actions and what was the impact on you.

- Script what you want to say and practice it.

First-Time Manager

"I'm losing sleep over being promoted to manager." Jeff did look bleary-eyed and added, "I'm a good geologist, but the least qualified in the company to supervise others. I know these guys, and most of them have more experience than I do."

Listen to Positive Comments; Don't Deflect Them

"What influenced you to take on this new role?" I asked.

There were several things. "In this culture, you don't turn down a promotion. And besides, I was getting bored with my job. My boss was convinced I'd be a good manager and thought I would make things better."

Jeff explained, "My idea of leadership is to be inclusive and to encourage others. I want to create a safe culture where we'd be open and honest. We'd tell each other what's working and what's not. For example, when someone was frustrating us, we'd tell him in a kind way. What happens now is we maintain harmony, but at the cost of getting results. We spend too much time on workarounds, trying not to offend anyone."

"Your ideas are both practical and caring," I told him. "The part I'm missing is why you doubt yourself."

He had doubts in three areas. "First, I'm not sure I can manage others. I don't know how to get off on the right foot.

"My second doubt is about getting along with my boss in this new position. Our relationship will be different. I'm concerned about getting time with him—he's so busy. I don't even have a job description.

"My third is, am I capable of implementing my leadership ideas? It's easy to talk about the changes but hard to implement. In listening to myself, I have to make a difference and try. These are the changes that motivated me to take the job."

Jeff was so modest I could hardly wait to point out his strengths. "Let's look at each of your concerns. Can you manage others? Your 360 feedback indicates you are in the top 20 percent in these categories: decisiveness, a quick study, compassion and sensitivity, self-awareness, and taking action.

"A few of the written comments were:

- Jeff is willing to stop what he is doing and help others even though it may negatively impact his projects.

- He knows the business and points out places where improvement can be made and does it in a way that isn't offensive.

- He says what needs to be said in a clear, direct way. He's a good communicator."

He had the qualities to be a good manager. Now, he just had to figure out how to get off on the right foot in his new role.

Jumpstart a Relationship with a New Boss or Coworker

I shared what I had learned that sets the right tone and jumpstarts relationships with subordinates. I recommended having individual meetings and saying something like this:

"We know each other, but as your supervisor, this will be a different relationship. Let me know how you want to be managed, so I don't have to guess. A good start is to describe the behaviors of the best boss you ever had.

"What did that boss do that resonated with you? I'll write these down and imitate them the best I can. I will try to remember what they are, but when I forget you have to remind me. If you're silent, then you're the problem, not me.

"Equally important is to reduce friction. What frustrates you? What are your hot buttons? If I know these I'll try to avoid pushing them. Again, I'll write these down, but if I forget, remind me. Your reminding me builds trust and keeps the relationship real. This is important.

"This should be reciprocal, so I'll describe ideal characteristics of some of the best people I've worked with, what they did that resonated with me, and I'll tell you my hot buttons."

I continued: "Your second concern is your new relationship with your boss. Consider having the same type of conversation with him as you will with the people reporting to you. You craft the conversation to fit in with how your boss thinks."

If You Don't Manage Up, You're the Problem

I stressed this was a key point. "Now that you have the foundation in place, it's your responsibility to manage up. Again, if you are silent, you are the problem. You and the people who support you will be overworked. Be specific about telling your boss the impact his requests have on you and your team. Bosses often have no idea of the cost of implementing requests. Your job is to give him man-hour costs for each request and tell him the impact it will have on other projects in terms of delays or quality. Do this and your team will know you have their backs. Don't do this and you'll be overwhelmed with requests.

"Don't wait for your boss or HR to give you a job description. Be proactive and draft one for him to use as a base document. This is a unique opportunity that you may never have again.

"Your third concern was your qualifications. You have good, positive thoughts and you have a heart for people. Set your mind on creating a safe, open, and honest culture each day. Be consistent and you'll have the impact you desire."

You Have Influence and Can Make a Difference

Jeff's reaction was a pleasant surprise. "I just realized my new position gives me influence with my boss and the people I work with and that I can make a difference. I come from the school of doing what I'm told. This shift in how I see things will open doors. I'm excited!"

JEFF'S TAKEAWAYS:

- I need to have one-on-one meetings with my new direct reports and set the tone.

- I need to have a conversation with my boss to set the tone.

- I will tell my boss the impact his requests have on the team. It's my job.

When Hard Work Doesn't Pay Off

··

"They won't promote me and I can't figure out why," Stephanie moaned. "I work hard, so I deserve a promotion. I'm motivated because I've been right-sized, downsized, and restructured four times. I vowed it wouldn't happen again, so I work hard. I don't waste time with chit-chat."

She was tense, talking in a staccato, rapid-fire way, and I wondered if there would ever be a pause. "If I go out to lunch, I find when I return to complete a task I've lost my train of thought and it takes time for me to rethink things. That is a waste of time, so I turn down lunch invitations."

When she finally took a breath, I asked, "What would you guess your reputation is in the company?"

She reflected briefly and said, "That I'm a no-nonsense, nose-to-the-grindstone, get-it-done person."

She said this with obvious professional pride and you could sense how clearly she saw this as her protection against future layoffs. I could also sense her fear.

Questions to Ponder

"If you were a worker bee, would you like to work for a grindstone boss?" was my first question. "Do you think those who are at the level where you aspire to be would welcome a person who is a recluse and unknown?"

We were on Skype, and this was the first time I'd seen her smile.

"I've never thought that hard work could send a negative message and that I've isolated myself," she said as the truth began to dawn on her. "I've been taught that hard work pays off and is its own reward."

I offered her something I'd heard: "Any strength used to excess takes on a cutting edge."

An "Aha" Moment

This hit her at a gut level. It was an epiphany—an "aha" moment. She began to realize the importance of relationships—of being seen as someone who is easy to work for and get along with. A person who makes the time to connect. Someone who is flexible, not rigid and driven.

How She Got Promoted, But...

Stephanie was determined to change and took action. She systematically bumped into people and would pause to talk; she invited others out to lunch, got to meetings early, and stayed late to chat. Six months later, she was promoted.

Everything seemed to have fallen into place, until her performance review. Her team was unhappy with the long hours and her demands for perfection. Her peers reported she was tense and less than cooperative.

For some reason, after the promotion, she had fallen back into her old habit of grinding out the work and not valuing relationships. We discussed the root of her obsession with work. She still carried the scars from previous layoffs and a fear of being unemployed.

A Boss Who Was Up-Front

Fortunately for Stephanie, a hard-nosed, tell-it-like-it-is boss came to her rescue. She took Stephanie aside, telling her that her obsession with work was derailing her. People were afraid to approach Stephanie, and if she continued to push her reports and peers for results without being more considerate, she was in danger of losing her job.

"Aha" Number Two

Stephanie was shocked. The very thing that she thought would ensure her success could get her fired. This was the second "aha" moment for Stephanie. She came to the conclusion that someone, or some force, was watching out for her.

In our next conversation, Stephanie said, "I don't play politics."

I quickly replied, "My issue with your using this over-used phrase is that it creates a negative frame of mind. How about changing your thinking to, 'People are important and relationships are important' instead of 'I don't play politics'? This is essential because paying attention to people first will get you the results you want."

STEPHANIE'S TAKEAWAYS:

- My hard work is a strength, but it is also my weakness.

- An important part of my boss's evaluation is not just the results, but how I get results. Do I care about others?

Surprise Leadership Lesson

It was a mild San Diego day with the early crowd settling in to chat before the speaker took the stage. I sat behind a mom, dad, three boys, and a young girl.

There was ample time for small talk, so I cleared my throat, hoping to get someone's attention. It worked, and as the girl in front turned I asked, "What's your name?"

"Lauren."

"How many children are in your family, Lauren?"

"There's me and my three brothers."

Lauren Turned My Small Talk into Big Talk

I wanted to keep the conversation alive. "Three brothers—how do you handle three brothers?"

I expected an offhand answer; instead, I received a tightly packed leadership lesson. "Easy," she said with a straight face, "You make them love you—then you can boss them around!"

I burst out laughing and was going to comment, but she turned her back to talk to her mother. That gave me time to think. She could use her "make them love you"—that is, caring about others to sweet-talk them, or the better path to create relationships.

To Judge Others Is to Miss Out on Wonderful Insights

Just then, a square-shouldered block of a man sat next to me. I'd met him at a breakfast a few months ago when he'd just been promoted to CEO.

Enthusiastically, I turned to the CEO and repeated what Lauren had said, emphasizing how caring for others can lead to the collaboration she got from her brothers. He either didn't hear me or, more likely, he dismissed the lesson because he turned his back on me to speak to someone else.

Emotions Trump Logic

I read his reaction, or lack of one, as similar to that of other leaders, including some doctors, lawyers, engineers, and other "in-your-head" folks, including myself, who are results-oriented and find emotions to be inconvenient—which is the way I used to think. I'll share my story because time has passed and I can laugh at myself.

I used to view emotions as a nuisance until a situation a number of years ago. Our teenage son was acting out. My approach was to impose strict boundaries and guidelines that had to be enforced. My wife's position was much more flexible and caring. This created so much tension between us that we sought the help of a counselor.

She listened to our take on the situation and I had to tell her my wife's response was totally emotional. The counselor said my wife's emotions were her logic. I immediately responded, "That's not logical!" The counselor's answer, which I've never forgotten, was, "Her emotions trump your logic."

I saw myself as a results-oriented, fact-based, logical, get-it-done person who had been hit by a disruptive concept. I learned that if people sense you don't care about them, then they won't listen to you. This has significantly improved my relationships.

Lauren's "Make Them Love You" Comment Trumps Defensiveness

I use Lauren's story of making them love you in certain coaching sessions. Her lesson is disarming because it makes cynical executives laugh out loud. It gets around their defenses, their ideas of reliance on reason, which are reflected in defensive statements I sometimes hear, such as:

"People should leave their problems at home."

"I tolerate small talk and telling others what you did on the weekend, but it is a waste of time."

"I'm trained to do a job, but I'm not good at the people stuff."

This last comment is a perfect example of self-deception. I don't think they realize that by saying, "I'm not good at the people stuff," they fail to own their responsibility to improve.

They are undermining their own job security and blocking the possibilities of promotion. A question that is always asked when someone is considered for a promotion is, "Does he get along with others?" Getting along is the people stuff.

See if this logic will help: Put some emotional capital in the bank, so when you frustrate a boss or coworker, you can make a withdrawal. Follow Lauren's advice and make them love you.

You Make Others Love You

How do you make others love you?

Start by writing down your definition of love. Not easy to do.

Now write down your three ideas of how to make others love you.

1. _____

2. _____

3. _____

I like this definition of love, which I mentioned in an earlier chapter: "It is to actively seek the welfare of another."

Let's unpack this definition. It is to think first of others, then yourself. Seeking welfare is doing small acts of kindness over a period of time. It is picking up someone's trash, offering a ride to a coworker whose car is in the shop, or sharing a lesson learned.

TAKEAWAYS:

- Make them love you.

- Wake up each day and ask yourself, "What will I do today to show others I'm seeking their welfare?"

Manage Others with a Business Case

I had started a company, and Charlie was in charge of our finance department. He worked long hours. There was constant turnover in accounting. He scrambled to stay staffed and he had no personal life, but he was about to change all of that with the stance he took—and he did it in one conversation.

Bosses Who Think They Have Great Ideas

Charlie was predictable, or so I thought. I guess that's why I remember what happened next. I approached him and said, "I want information on *X*." I can't remember exactly what I asked for, but my requests for information were frequent.

I expected Charlie to tell me he'd get right on it, but that's not what happened. He said, "Let me think about it and I'll get back to you in an hour."

Surprised, I walked back to my office and wasn't sure what to think. That was not Charlie's normal reaction.

Respectfully Present the Data

An hour later, Charlie came into my office. "I've thought about your request. It will take thirty man-hours at a fully loaded overhead cost of $120.00 per hour for a total of $3,600 to get your information."

I was incredulous. "You've got to be kidding me. You're exaggerating. My request is not that complex. I can't believe it will cost anywhere near that amount!"

Charlie didn't succumb to my emotions; rather, he stuck to business. "The cost is $3,600. It's your company. You're the boss. If that's what you want, that's what we'll do."

Charlie calmly continued. "There is more. I looked into the impact your request would have on two projects we're currently working on. The first project will be delayed by two days and the second by half a day."

I sat forward in my chair, beginning to get upset. "Those two projects are important and I don't want them delayed. I am not happy with what I'm hearing. Once again, I think you're exaggerating. What I'm asking for is not that much and I'm irritated."

Charlie didn't react. He simply said, "It's your company. I'll do what you ask, but I needed to tell you the impact of the request."

Alone in my office, after I'd cooled down, Charlie's earlier comment came back to me "Let me think about it and I'll get back to you." Now I had to think about my request. I asked myself this question: "If I had the data I'm looking for in my hands, would it save me money or make me money?"

The answer was irritating because the data would do neither. The data was simply something I wanted, and my frame of mind was that I wanted it because I wanted it. I'd never weighed the cost or considered the impact on others. I went back to Charlie and told him I had changed my mind, and I did not need the information. I then thanked him. It took guts for him to do what he did, and I knew I needed his feedback going forward.

You Can Educate Them and Make Your Job Easier

Charlie's approach taught me to consider how my requests would impact both company finances and the staff. The result was my requests decreased, Charlie's hours decreased, and the turnover in the accounting department decreased.

I use the Charlie story a lot when coaching, noting that nowhere in our conversation did he use the standard objections of telling me that he was overwhelmed, nor did he tell me he needed additional manpower, nor did he talk about either himself or his team being burned out.

Instead, Charlie was respectful and he left me in control. The final decision was mine to make.

When I pushed back and got upset, he remained silent. He let that silence do the heavy lifting. He limited his comments to the business case, the cost, and the impact on other projects. He was not drawn in to my emotions.

Ask yourself, how can I manage and enlighten my superiors about the impact their requests have on limited resources in a way they can hear it? You might influence them if they knew how excessive requests affected product quality or diminished customer service.

MY TAKEAWAYS:

- As bosses, we are often the problem—not our employees.

- As bosses, do we create a safe environment where people can tell us the impact of our assignments?

- As employees, how we speak up is important. Presenting an issue as solely a business matter takes the emotion out of the discussion.

- As employees and as bosses, if we are overworked, we are part of the problem.

- As employees, ask yourselves if being quiet is working for you.

Want Feedback with Value? Be Specific

....

"People who do good work get laid off. It's politics. I'm a scientist, not a politician, and that makes me nervous." Max and I were in a small conference room for a coaching session.

I Can't Improve If I Don't Know What to Improve

He leaned back. "By politics I mean it's who figures out how to get along with the key players. I don't know if I'm getting along or not. I need feedback. How do I get it?"

"Have you ever asked for feedback," I inquired, "and do you know how to ask for it?"

He answered no to both.

I asked, "What do you want feedback on? Do you want it on you the scientist, you the person, or you as part of the leadership team?"

"First, I want feedback on their impressions of me personally. Am I seen as flexible and approachable? Then on me the scientist/team member, to see if they think I contribute in meaningful ways and am doing my job."

I told him to reflect for a moment. "Before you ask someone for feedback, play the role of the feedback giver. If someone asked you for the kind of feedback you want, would you give it?"

A long pause. "I'm fearful of giving feedback. Even if I can get past the anxiety, it depends on what they are asking and how they ask. The relationship may be at stake, so it's easier to go softly."

An Idea on How to Ask for Feedback

Max's answers made him aware he was seeking information about himself that would make his coworkers uneasy.

I offered this thought: "Here's what makes feedback easier to ask for and easier for others to provide. If you suspect there is an area where you could improve, you ask for their input on this specific area."

It makes people uncomfortable to ask a wide open question such as, "What do you think I should work on to be more effective?" This puts them in a position of judging you.

"Here is an example—picture this in your mind. Mike comes to you and says, 'I think I lose people in conversations and I'm not sure why. What one or two suggestions do you have on how you've seen others improve?'"

"That makes sense. Asking in this way would reduce my anxiety." Max said, "What I like is the other person has approached me. Mike was clear on what he wanted. Now I can see how I can get feedback doing the same thing. Approach them and be specific. This method lowers the risk."

"You got it!" I said, adding, "When you get feedback, thank them. Avoid the temptation to improve on their suggestions or drag the conversation out.

"Skeptics in the feedback process see asking for feedback and self-improvement resolutions as hollow. Overcome this and bring them along with you by saying, 'It will be hard for me to change and I will need your help. Be my mirror. Reflect back to me when I'm following your suggestions and when I don't. Your feedback about my behavior is key to my change.

"What you are doing is involving them on an ongoing basis. So often we think in terms of one-and-done, such as reading a book or going to a workshop. Changing behavior or breaking a habit takes repetition, with correction, over a longer period. Capturing feedback on an ongoing basis is your quality control loop.

"Max, you're a scientist," I said, with a smile. "You do an experiment, look at the results and try again. Do the same with people. You need to know the results or impact you have on the people you work with."

Another benefit of feedback is to improve and strengthen your job security. Losing a job is a fear that can be overcome by your knowing how you are doing versus waiting for a distant future performance review or simply hoping you're O.K.

MAX'S TAKEAWAYS:

- I will make my best guess on areas I need to work on and go to others to ask for their suggestions on how to improve.

- People like to give advice, and I can open the door so they can freely make suggestions.

- If there are times I'm not prepared to ask for feedback, I will ask myself "why not?"

21

I'm Overwhelmed

....

"I'm overwhelmed."

Jen was well practiced at playing one song on a one-string guitar. "I'm overwhelmed. I work ten to twelve hours a day, but can't keep up with all the work."

This song seems to be catching on, and it's worth exploring the impact on musician and audience.

Jen was in finance—a key position—so the impact this song had on the president of the company and other team members was significant. It created uncertainty, undermining Jen's own security. They began to question why it took so long to do her job, whether or not she could do the job, and the impact long hours would have on her health.

They May Reject Your Offer to Help

The management team knew her, liked her, and wanted her to succeed. One team member, Amanda, said she thought she could help, so she sent an e-mail proposing a date and time to talk. Later she said, "Jen didn't respond. I had tried to schedule meetings before so I wasn't surprised, but I was disappointed."

Amanda still wanted to help. "I didn't give up and we finally met. I suggested we should come in on a Saturday to see what we could come up with. We would list the requirements of her job along with estimated man-hours and see how they matched up to the resources in her department. She should then take this to the president and have a concrete discussion. Maybe the facts would support an additional person.

"Jen told me it sounded like a good idea. I offered a Saturday meeting more than once, but she never accepted my offer. I knew she had been looking for another job, so I wasn't surprised when I found out that she had accepted a new one."

To Intervene or Not?

She paused. "I have been thinking about this and doing some soul-searching. Jen was a team member and we let her down. I tried to help, but she was in a downward spiral and headed for a crash. She saw another job as her only alternative."

Amanda took a deep breath. "I should have done an intervention! The president should have had a serious conversation with her and done a gap analysis of problems and solutions. Then he should either have come alongside or found her help."

She stared into the future and said, "Team members should take care of each other. That means having tough conversations and coming alongside people in a caring and proactive way. They should go the extra mile for each other."

Face Your Problem—Resolve it or It Will Follow You Everywhere You Go

I went into coach mode and reflected on Jen leaving with a victim mindset instead of being proactive and asking herself, "What can I do to not be so overwhelmed?" Jen may now have a good job, but her problem went with her, and it's only a matter of time until she will once again feel overwhelmed.

It seems you are doomed to repeat life's lessons until you get it right, change your behavior, and finally pass the course.

TAKEAWAYS JEN NEVER GOT AT THIS JOB:

- Grumbling and complaining create doubt in the minds of those around you and they begin to question your capabilities. Can she carry the load? How is she impacting our success?

- Face your challenges where you are as quickly as you can. Ignoring reality doesn't work.

TAKEAWAYS FOR AMANDA:

- Next time if someone continues to complain and not change, I'll say, "If you want to complain, pay a psychologist to listen to you. If you will work at changing, I'd like to help."

COACH'S COMMENT:

- If after multiple attempts to help someone you find you're more interested in helping him or her improve than he or she is, don't stop caring about others, but consider finding someone else you can help.

It Isn't All About Book Knowledge

Here I am I'm writing a book, and I say it isn't all about book knowledge. The operative word is *all*. Read on and you'll get the point that it is what you do with this knowledge that determines the outcome.

You would expect a CPA firm made up of well-educated, business-savvy people to invest in their employees. The managing partner I coached struggled with how to do this.

He told me he found the answer. He said, "We are on the right track—I bought everyone in the firm the book *Good to Great*. We'll all read it, and we are good to go."

Employees often see buying a book as the flavor-of-the-month, since there is generally no follow-through, nor is there long-term commitment. The CPA firm didn't invest in their employees' development, so turnover increased and morale was low. It wasn't a surprise when they were absorbed by a larger firm.

Does the Educational Model of "Buy Them a Book" Work?

You would expect the gray-haired general manager of an electronics firm with an MBA and a stack of books on leadership to know how to develop a high-functioning team. The problem was in his mind—once he'd read a good leadership book, it was as if he'd implemented what he read. He didn't seek feedback, and it was even sadder yet to see that his team was fearful of volunteering feedback.

It's a Lot about Relationships

Now contrast the first two examples with the following—a Venture Capital (VC) firm. You would expect a VC firm to deal with their employees in a detached, by-the-numbers manner.

But the managing partners of this VC firm knew they had to make a long-term commitment to enhance book knowledge in order to build a culture of concern, collaboration, and trust. They were market-savvy, knowing this would separate them from the competition since companies looking for financing from a VC would be looking for more than just the money. All VCs had money.

That was the borrower perspective. The investors in the VC fund wanted to see a cohesive VC team before investing. The VC firm knew collaboration would happen through building relationships with one another.

Bullet Point List They Used to Know They Were Investing in Relationships

You are investing in relationships if:

- you make the time to connect
- you show respect and value each person
- you stop what you are doing and invite someone to sit down
- you are fully present
- you ask questions to go deeper

Making the time to know someone often results in making allowances.

How do you get to know someone? Good questions equal good conversations.

The getting-to-know-you process in the VC firm was jumpstarted with an e-mail that assigned rotating lunch and coffee meetings for everyone, which included three questions each team member would answer:

1. Where is your favorite place to take out-of-town guests?

2. What does "success" mean to you?

3. What in this world breaks your heart?

Getting to know a coworker diminishes the tendency to be judgmental and heightens empathy. It adds elasticity and willingness to be forgiving and gives people the second chance we'd all like.

You're a Mess and So Am I

The VC firm acknowledged human fallibility and imperfections. The reality was there would be disconnects, friction, and mutual frustration. There would be times to have difficult conversations, but more often it was advisable to minimize or make allowances for another's faults to preserve relationships.

TAKEAWAYS:

- Good relationships require attention to others

- Good relationships make you want to come to work

- Relationships planted and watered bear fruit

COACH'S COMMENT:

- Treat people as if they already are what they can become.

- FYI: The VC firm is prospering and growing.

A Two-For: Almost Fired to Awards; Irritation to Collaboration

A red-faced Jo told me, "I'm on the leadership team. The two best-educated and highest-paid employees are the two biggest underperformers. They are male. I have to work harder to outperform them because I don't have a college degree and I'm a female. These guys should learn what Claire, my direct report, learned."

It seemed best to let Jo cool down and I was curious. "Tell me what Claire learned that you hope they will learn and tell me how she learned it."

From Almost Fired to a Performance Award

Jo's face lit up. "Claire is an engineer who stepped on people's toes and was clueless about it. Everyone she bumped into had an 'ouch' reaction and I heard about it. I suggested they tell Claire what was going on and they all said, 'No way.'"

Jo explained her dilemma. "It took me six months to find and train Claire, so if I wanted to keep her, I had to figure out how to motivate her to change. I couldn't fix her—she had to do that herself. If I couldn't work through this, I'd have to find a replacement.

"I told Claire there were two parts to her job. One was to provide technical support to her internal customers. The other was to get along with them. She got an *A* on technical support and an *F* on getting along. I told her that the job required both and I wanted her to keep her job. She told me she liked the job.

"We had a serious talk and I told her I'd coach her on people skills, but only if she was committed to the pain of self-examination and change. Claire agreed. I felt apprehensive because I knew Claire to be stubborn, but she suddenly became compliant. My doubts were allayed when she explained that she'd struggled with relationships all her life and had no idea how to improve them."

Enlist Peers to Help

Jo explained that Claire, being the classic engineer, wanted concrete evidence of the problem. Jo went to the people Claire had interacted with. She made it crystal clear to them that if they lost Claire, they lost valuable technical expertise. She quickly added she had prepared Claire to listen to feedback. It was their responsibility to tell Claire the exact behavior that bothered them, the impact, and how they wanted Claire to change.

Move Beyond You; Focus on Helping Them

Before all this could happen, Jo told me she had forced herself to look beyond her prejudices about Claire, the better-educated engineer making more money, to the higher purpose of helping Claire. The empathy really kicked in when she realized Claire had never had anyone come alongside to help and that she'd struggled with relationships all her life.

Jo was persistent and very patient with Claire. Over a period of time, relationships improved, as did business results—so much so that Claire received a merit award for the most improved employee in the engineering department.

I commended Jo. "You have told me a great story. It has a circular quality. You started off telling me about the two teammates who were underperformers. You just told me about Claire the underperformer and how you put aside your prejudices, got to know her, empathized with her inability to form relationships, and coached her to new levels."

They Should Know Better, but They Don't, So Help Them

"You've probably helped others in the same way. Do you recognize that you have a gift of moving people from stuck to unstuck? How about helping your two teammates? Your motivation can be twofold—to help because it makes business sense and because it's the right thing to do. Simply do with them what you did with Claire. Set aside your prejudices and get to know them."

Her reaction was the expression you get on your face when you know you should do something but you really don't want to do it. Her prejudices were so strong that she just couldn't see a reason to help these guys. She needed to find motivation from a different place.

I went deeper. "Are you open and collaborative with your two teammates, or are you tense and guarded?" I didn't wait for her answer. "Your attitude is guarded and shut down. You can change your attitude by forgiving the comments made that wounded you and helping them the same way you helped Claire. You have a choice to make. Forgive them or let it eat at you."

Jo did not make an immediate decision. There was a battle going on in her head. The dilemma was resolved when one of the guys had a blow-up with the boss. While in a state of shock, he mentioned the incident to Jo, who sat down with him over coffee and talked about how to resolve the issue. He acknowledged her emotional intelligence was higher than his. He followed her advice and there was reconciliation.

She never became friends with her male teammates, but there was collaboration and she gained some inner peace.

JO'S TAKEAWAY:

- Coaching someone to success is rewarding.

- Move beyond irritation to collaboration.

- Forgiveness heals the wound.

An Introvert Struggles to Be a Manager

A joke I heard about actuaries will help you understand Kim.

Question: Do you know how to tell an extroverted actuary from an introverted actuary? Answer: An extroverted actuary looks at your shoes when talking to you.

Introverted actuary Kim and I met. She said, "I'm not sure which is more painful—becoming a manager or my not having analyzed the job of manager before I accepted it."

In advance of our meeting, I looked up the definition of actuary: "One who analyzes the potential for undesirable events to occur and helps to plan for (or avoid) those events."

The definition helped me understand why she was upset with herself for accepting the promotion before analyzing the job. Once in the job, she found she had to leave her comfort zone to make the stretch from individual contributor to manager.

Understand the Job before You Accept It

I asked Kim to tell me what she was wrestling with. She named her top three issues:

1. You need to be engaged at all times.
2. You are expected to make decisions based on details you may not fully understand, and often without *any* details.

3. You have to ask clarifying questions, but she felt asking questions makes you look weak.

I asked for her top one. "You need to be engaged at all times."

"What is the impact of being engaged?" I asked, knowing full-on engagement would be difficult for an introvert.

She had a ready answer: "I'm a battery that is drained by going to one meeting after another. Before my promotion, I'd go to meetings, sit there, and half-listen. I could coast to conserve energy. I'm no longer just an observer and have to engage my entire mind. There is also the pressure to say something, but I'm not always sure of what to say."

Relations at home were strained too. "At the end of the day I have no desire to talk to my husband and I'm cranky with our children. I'm drained."

I found myself scrambling to think of something that would help. "Let's start with your last comment. What if you told your husband and the kids what you told me—that you were like a battery and your energy was drained before you got home? That you know you are on edge after work and not pleasant to be around and you don't like being that person. Your solution could be that you will try to recharge before you come home by leaving work early to work out.

"There might be times you can't work out, so you will take a walk instead and be fifteen minutes later than usual. If they'd understand this, their reward would be a kinder, gentler you."

Tell Them Who You Are

"Consider using a similarly open and honest approach with people at work who need to understand you, so they won't be surprised when you take a break. Some thoughts are to walk the halls or go outside, let cold water run over your hands and splash some on your face, or even hide out and play games on your phone."

Then I addressed her other two challenges. "You are expected to make decisions based on details you may not fully understand and often without any details at all, and you have to ask clarifying questions. The problem you said is that this makes you look weak."

Questions Are Your Best Friends

I suggested she look to Voltaire. He wrote, "Judge a man by his questions rather than his answers." As an introvert, she had the advantage of thinking before speaking, to form good questions. I advised, "If you need more information before making a decision, ask questions. If you are in a meeting and know you should contribute, ask a question."

What Are the Positives of Your Job?

We were spending too much time on the negatives of being a manager, so I asked, "What's been good about being a manager?"

She gave me a big smile. "My team is my rock. They all have good intentions. I am proud of their work. We get involved in exciting projects to help the company avoid undesirable events."

KIM'S TAKEAWAYS:

- Be comfortable with you. Being someone else is already taken.

- Help people understand you by telling them who you are.

Straight Talk and Performance

Debbie is a dynamo, full of energy and enthusiasm. She leads a team of fifteen employees. Matt is young and a top performer with the potential to succeed her, but he rubs people the wrong way. He is self-absorbed. No one on the team wants him as their future leader.

I asked Debbie if she had talked to Matt about this and she said she had. He didn't seem to get the message that if all he wanted was to be an individual contributor he was doing fine; if he wanted to lead a team, however, he had to turn the dimmer down on himself and turn it up to spotlight the team. It was not all about him; it was all about the team. She added that when she delivered the message to Matt, she avoided conflict and wasn't direct enough.

It's Not About Conflict; It's About Performance and Helping Them

I told her to hold on a minute. "You just provided Matt with invaluable feedback for his career. You said you have difficulty with conflict. Your conversation was not about conflict. Recast your thinking—Matt has a blind spot. As his manager, you have an obligation to point this out and how it will affect his future.

"Give him some examples of his behavior when he is focused on himself, and then contrast this with how he might behave if he cared about others. He can then make a choice to change and appreciate having you coach him to a promotion."

Debbie listened, nodded, and then diagnosed his problem. "His mind is set on building a reputation of being right and driving for results. He is blind to the impact on others. Apparently, he believes as long as he delivers he's done his job."

She continued, "I will talk to Matt about what it takes to be promoted within my department. I believe people are an amazing creation and we need to treat each other with respect regardless of age, gender, or education. I'll make it clear that valuing others is how you build a high-performing team."

DEBBIE'S TAKEAWAYS:

- Tell the team the culture revolves around respect for one another.

- My job is to tell team members if they are not performing, and sooner not later.

My Work Is My Identity

This is the second part of Debbie's story from chapter 25. She asked if we could change the subject from Matt to herself. She wanted to discuss balance in her life. We talked about work, which she loved, and she concluded that since she loved work, balance was a minor issue. I wasn't buying this—after all, she had brought it up in the first place.

I asked her to describe friendships and relationships she had outside of work. She began to tear up and admitted they were nonexistent.

As if to dull the pain, she rationalized her loneliness by saying she got great satisfaction when her boss gave her a project and she made the project happen. We talked about how she continued to get involved in project after project. She teared up again, as she talked about how this led to a cycle of nothing but work.

My Work Is My Identity

Her eyes got wide, then she burst out with, "I just realized why I'm a work addict. I can't say no. I desperately want to be liked. But there is more. My competency and work are my identity. If I don't work hard, my identity is threatened. I am my work."

There was a very long pause, which yielded a surprise result. It dawned on her: "I am the problem. It's not outside pressures. It's me!" This admission thrilled her.

We laughed and I said, "It's got to be comforting to know you're the problem and you can give yourself permission to solve it."

You Can't Have All Your Needs Met at Work

We discussed how she could have her needs met outside of work. She named four people she'd like to build relationships with and ended by saying, "I never find the time to be with caring friends. I must make the time."

She described her dependence on work for self-esteem, like being a chip of wood in an ocean tossed up then down with each passing wave. She believed if she were centered, the happy-to-sad peaks and valleys would diminish. With hope in her voice, she told me her quest was to find inner peace.

DEBBIE'S TAKEAWAYS:

- The quest for inner peace is worthy. With help, I'll get there.

- My work is my identity...if I lose my job, will I cease to exist?

- Admitting I'm a workaholic was hard.

- I want a few close friends to truly care about me.

People Lead to Results

"On the flight to San Diego, I was tired and decided to stop work and reflect," Meg shared. "I was struck by my attitude toward my mother and sister. I don't make time to improve either relationship, nor do I make time for people at work. It's all about me and what I need."

Meg was in human resources, so I expected her to be outgoing, but I didn't expect such honesty or self-awareness. Her vulnerability set the tone for a rich conversation as I wondered what would come next.

Our meeting was a coaching session to review feedback from boss, peers, and direct reports so she could learn more about herself.

A Paradox

We went over the results. There was a paradox in the comments. Some said she was cold and intense, others said she put them at ease and was a warm, caring person.

Meg explained, "The paradox comes because when I'm focused on an outcome, it's all about getting results. When I take a deep breath and slow down, I'm naturally empathetic and care for people."

My impression was she'd just now realized she separated the two. Out of curiosity, I asked, "Do you see these as contradictory?"

"I haven't given it any thought," she mused. "A given is you have to have outcomes or results. Less obvious and perhaps harder is to be caring."

Default Is to Go for Results

"The best answer," she said, "would be if you could get results and care about people at the same time. That doesn't mean that's what I'll do, because when I'm under pressure my default thinking is only about results."

"Meg, are you aware of a pattern in the comments you've made about yourself?" I asked.

She wasn't.

"You are real with yourself," I explained. "It is rare that someone is as open and honest as you. Most of us are defensive. You have chosen the path to improvement by owning your selfishness, that you are the problem with your mother and sister."

I went on. "You also said you can get results and care about people but admitted under pressure you will go for results."

In a faltering voice, she said, "I know I've got to stop taking from my family and start giving, which I think I can do, but changing my behavior in the company will be harder. The emphasis at work is more on the results than on the people."

She shifted in her chair, looked at me, and said, "I have a clear picture that I am both the problem and the solution and I'm okay with that; however, if people feel I'm more focused on me than them, I don't know how to change that perception."

How Do You Change a Perception?

I agreed. Perceptions are hard to change, so I shared with her what had worked for others. I suggested she talk to a couple of confidants and tell them the specific behaviors she wanted to change, then enlist them as her change partners.

"Own your 'stuff.' Say to your confidants something like, 'In the past, my automatic reaction is to think of *me* and what *I* want to be done. The new me wants my first reaction to be engaging others to understand them first and then to discuss the project.'"

Ask for Their Help

I suggested she tell them, "I need help. I can't observe myself, so I won't know if I'm changing or not. Be my video camera and play back my behavior. Let me know—did you witness me focusing on results first or others first?"

"By doing this," I assured her, "you're inviting them to take off their old glasses and put on new ones to observe you in a different way. Your vulnerability will be genuine and you'll establish stronger relationships."

I ended the conversation by asking what she'd learned.

She said that her "aha" moment came because she was on a plane, quiet, and not working, which left space for the universe to speak to her about her family. "I can't explain why, but for some reason, I was open and saw that I was the problem. That makes it hard and easy at the same time. Hard because it was me and I was blind. Easy because I can fix it."

"What else did you learn?"

"Asking for help can be a strength if you are sincere and will change. You can be more approachable and be a model for others who are too results-oriented."

Meg paused and added, "You can't change yourself—you need both support and a mirror to reflect back your behavior. I've wondered why my self-help efforts had yielded feeble results. Going forward I have a new model; however, it is humbling."

MEG'S TAKEAWAY:

. . . .

- I have a better understanding of how people lead to results.

- My default setting is results.

- I can look at myself and not get defensive.

- You can change perceptions.

Five Questions Used to Assess You

You would expect a female CFO in a male-dominated company to be primarily numbers-oriented in order to fit into the traditional CFO mold.

Live Inside-Out

Meet Brittany, the unusual CFO, the mother of two teenagers, who does volunteer work for local charities while balancing her corner-office duties. Her inner strength comes from living life inside-out, trusting in the divine, and the love of her family and friends.

In our coaching sessions, I experienced her inner strength through her relaxed demeanor and smiles. It's liberating to be with someone who is real, who isn't trying to make an impression. She figured out to be effective, you have to move beyond self and misdirected competitiveness.

Brittany made this transition, so I felt invited into the conversations, which is her secret sauce for relationships. It's what distinguishes her and is a significant reason why she was promoted to CFO.

Brittany the Difference Maker, and You as a Difference Maker

Here is how her secret sauce saved an employee from being fired.

As I sat down for a coaching session in her office, I asked, "Brittany, what's on your mind?"

"Sue, the new hire, is on my mind. Remember I told you I hired her based on a friend's recommendation and that she was not living up to my expectations? I told you I was going to let her go."

During a previous session, I suggested Brittany ask herself, "Can I keep Sue and give her a second chance? Can I become a blank sheet of paper and interview her a second time?" The answer was she could, so this is what she did.

"I asked Sue about her prior experience, specifically in two key areas where her performance was lacking," Brittany said. "She's had hardly any experience in either of these areas. The obvious explanation was I had assumed she had experience because I'd had a recommendation."

I Am the Problem, Not Her

Brittany looked me in the eye and said, "I blew it. I'm the problem, not Sue."

She continued. "I swallowed hard at this reevaluation and forced myself to put me aside and remember I owed her a second chance. I pulled out the five questions I use to evaluate employees."

You can use the same questions to assess yourself and understand how others are assessing you and increase the odds of retention and promotion.

1. Does she listen and hear what is being said?

2. Does she have a positive attitude?

3. Is she coachable?

4. Is she a quick learner?

5. Can she get along with others?

Brittany said, "Sue is a good listener, she has a positive upbeat attitude, she is coachable, a quick learner, and is well-liked because she's always helping others.

"Sue has upside potential. We know her, and it is good business to invest in her growth. Plus, we don't have to look for a replacement. She wins, the company wins, and I win."

BRITTANY'S TAKEAWAYS:

- I can admit my mistakes.

- My list of five questions is good. I will stick to it.

- I can be both approachable and hold people accountable.

29

Functioning When It's Dysfunctional

....

The company was under pressure to reduce costs. The head of the human resources department had publicly stated that salaries and benefits were good, so if any employee was not satisfied, he or she should look for a job elsewhere.

This short-term mindset of reducing costs by reducing the number of employees impacted Bob's group. Bob was the manager of a group of fifteen. For the past five years, Bob's group had been asked each year to reduce head count by one person.

Keep Your Head Down

Bob said, "The way we dealt with this was to keep our heads down and be invisible. The halls were quiet and conversations muffled. Whatever collaboration and synergy that had existed before disappeared."

We talked briefly about ways of changing the overall environment, but this was neither practical nor actionable, due in part to the asinine statement from the head of human resources. So we shifted the conversation to what Bob could do.

Be a Victor Not a Victim

"Bob, tell me how you see management and the impact it has on you and the team."

His response was, "Management's position is, 'My way or the highway.' My reaction and that of the team is to do enough work to get by and limit the interaction with management."

"I'm curious—how is that working?"

Bob had obviously thought about this. "It's a way to get through the day. The thing that isn't working is our sense of satisfaction and personal growth."

"That sounds grim. I'll ask the obvious question: 'What can you do to get job satisfaction, grow personally, and be a role model for the team?'"

I quickly added, "The purpose of my question is to move you from being self-focused to team-focused, from being passive and negative to proactive and positive."

Bob said his response would surprise me and it did. "I've had flashes of what I need to do to lead the team, becoming energized, and have even had moments visualizing how we can stun management with our accomplishments."

He stared out the window and said, "It's fun to daydream, but to accomplish the dream takes work and commitment. That's the execution piece. My boss says I'm weak on execution. I wasn't sure what he meant, so I looked up execution, and it means the carrying out or putting into effect of a plan. He is right. So, though I would like to stun management, I don't have a plan and I'm not committed."

"Do you plan on working here for another five or ten years?" I asked.

"No," he replied.

"Do you think in your next job you'll have to execute?"

"Yes."

I looked at him. "How are you going to learn to execute and then practice it if you don't start now? You have a job and are being paid to execute; therefore, you have a scholarship to learn how to execute. You should jump on this opportunity and get trained for your next job."

Bob took a class in project management. There was a project the company was pushing him to complete, but the progress was slow. He realized he could apply what he was learning to this project.

He met with each team member and went over their responsibilities. Then he put together a chart with team member names and the individual responsibilities. The chart showed how team members were to interact with each other, and it included timelines and milestones.

The team was energized with Bob's leadership, and management was surprised by an on-time completion.

Bob used what he learned from this in an interview for another job. The interview went well because he pointed out how his team performed under difficult circumstances. This landed him the job—one that was more rewarding.

BOB'S TAKEAWAYS:

- I do have a scholarship, but I never looked at work that way.

- There is more risk in not executing than in executing.

- The gift is to know I have a weakness and deal with it.

Reluctant Boss Invests in Employee

....

Hard-driving Steve was promoted twice in nine months. He believed he'd be promoted a third time if he could recruit Roberta from a competitor.

He saw his competitor as soft and weak, so Roberta would excel working for him. Steve offered Roberta more money and coaxed her into joining his team.

As we sat in his office he told me, "Roberta is a bust. She is tense and fragile; worse yet, not productive."

I asked him why he'd hired Roberta. His clipped answer was, "I needed an extra pair of hands and feet to implement my ideas."

That comment pushed a hot button of mine. "Steve, you told me in a prior conversation you liked direct feedback. Here it comes. If Roberta were a robot and implemented your ideas, would that be a good thing?"

I didn't wait for his answer. "Roberta is a person you're treating like a robot."

He stared at me. "What's your point?"

"I'd guess your meetings are rushed," I said, working to calm my voice. "You do most of the talking, which involves your directives.

I'm thinking to myself, he can dish it out—let's see if he can take it.

His reaction was, "That was harsh." There was a pause before he said, "There may be some truth to what you said. It's obvious that what I'm doing isn't working. Roberta is passive and not productive. What would you suggest?"

"A couple of things, starting with treating Roberta the same way you would like to be treated. Then assume all your interactions with Roberta are instantly put on YouTube, along with your name."

He nodded for me to continue.

"Next, do you think she knows what you want and feels safe in executing on what you require?"

He was paying attention because he paused to think before answering.

"No, I don't think she does. I rush and haven't been clear about what I want. My attitude is I'm paying her top dollar and I don't have time to babysit."

Steve read my mind, "You don't have to tell me—I'll lose that attitude. I'll make the time to be clear about what I want, when I want it, decisions she can make, and I'll set up progress meetings with her."

He continued, "I doubt she feels safe. I just wanted the work to get done. I'm beginning to realize her value. I need to think more about her needs, or I'll be spending time finding a replacement."

This was a perfect opening. "You can hit the reset button with Roberta by owning the problems you've caused. Steve, I'll model the conversation you should have. You'd better record it."

Roberta, I've given you a lot of responsibility on key projects. My guess is you are more concerned about not making mistakes than getting the job done. You're new and will make mistakes early on and I can live with that. You may not believe me, but I'll demonstrate I have your back. I've been a problem in another way. I haven't paused to work with you to lay out a step-by-step plan for each project, nor have I asked for your input. I have to make the time and help you plan so you'll succeed. I realized that if I don't support you, then you may leave the company, which would be my fault and my loss. I hope we can push through this rough patch.

I doubted Steve heard the changes he needed to make, so I asked him to recap key points. After three iterations, this is what he came up with.

STEVE'S TAKEAWAYS:

- I was focused on self and my needs to the exclusion of Roberta, which almost drove her away.

- Leadership isn't all about me. It has to include others. Others make it happen.

- Treat people as if they already are what they can become.

To Influence, You Must Speak Up

Juan Jose (J.J.) received this feedback from his boss: "You don't have an opinion. You don't speak up. You would rather get along with everyone than get the job done."

The Quandary of Being Liked

J.J.'s story magnifies a common quandary of wanting to be liked while knowing it's often at the expense of getting results.

J.J. strives for harmony. An alarm bell sounds in his head with confrontational situations or uncomfortable conversations.

He is in sales and said, "Customers buy from people they like. This fits with who I am—I want to be liked. I am quick to meet customers' requests."

J.J. took a deep breath. "My boss is right. My need to be liked has affected my work. I am too accommodating."

In a resigned tone, J.J. added, "My boss sees me as an ineffective communicator because I talk around issues to avoid conflict, I don't speak up, and I'm not decisive."

"J.J., may I share my thoughts?" He agreed. "You are indecisive because you care for people. If you suppress your caring for people, it will have a negative impact on relationships and on your sales."

"Keep your caring about people and add the missing piece. Your boss did a good job of diagnosing the missing piece, which is to speak up."

I'm thinking to myself, J.J. knows he needs to speak up, but will he? So I asked, "Can you give me a good reason you'll speak up?"

Why Change?

J.J. said that his boss was a well-connected mentor who would back him in a potential promotion to a new team that had the responsibility of restructuring the future of the company. J.J. would be in the inner circle. However, if J.J. didn't change, there would be no promotion.

I gave J.J. a role-play test to see if he could speak up.

"J.J., here is a hypothetical situation. It's time for lunch. You and Henry go to a salad bar nearby. Henry tells you he has a presentation to his boss after lunch and he's nervous. You walk back to the office after lunch and you notice Henry has a black speck stuck between his front teeth.

I asked, "What do you do?

- Do you hope someone else will tell Henry before his meeting?

- Do you tell yourself he'll see it in a mirror?

- Do you tell him there is something between his teeth?"

J.J. was honest and said, "I think I'd tell him, but I'm not sure."

"Would you like to be sure?" I asked. "Would you like to develop a conditioned response to speaking up?"

He nodded yes, so I continued. "You have to train to speak up just as you have to train to run a marathon. Your training starts with training your mind. Paste this list in two places you'll see every day:

1. Speaking up is a skill I can learn.

2. I will be promoted if I speak up.

3. I will have a voice and be valued.

4. My caring about and wanting to help others trumps my fear of speaking up.

5. Speaking up is an attitude I will put on daily."

J.J. asked me to give an example of speaking up that circumvented defensiveness.

"Let's go back to Henry, who has something between his teeth. With your new mindset of speaking up, you don't hesitate— you stop Henry and say, 'Henry, if I had something between my teeth and was about to give a presentation would you tell me?'

"He'd have to say yes, so then you say: 'Henry, you have something between your teeth.'"

J.J. burst out laughing.

The two underlying principles are:

1. "Do unto others as you would have them do unto to you."

2. If someone gets upset, you explain your intent was to help him or her and you hope he or she would do the same for you. When feedback is reciprocal, it mitigates your fears and adds balance.

J.J.'s final question was, "You said I'd have to train to speak up. How will I know I'm in training?"

"You'll know you are speaking up when you are uncomfortable," I replied. "If a day passes and you've been comfortable, then you haven't practiced speaking up."

J.J.'S TAKEAWAYS:

- Speaking up is a skill I can learn and must learn.

- I learn by repetition, so I'll memorize the five-point list.

- I will select two people and tell them my goal is to speak up and have them observe me and give me feedback.

32

Performance Problems and a Possible Solution

· ·

I have strong beliefs about performance problems and how they should be handled.

Here is why. I was consulting with a firm that was letting five employees go. They held a meeting and told them that due to economic circumstances, their jobs were eliminated and that at the end of the meeting they would meet with an outside resource that would help them in finding a new job. They were handed a schedule with my name, times to meet, and the location.

I was assigned an office and met with each person to see how they were taking the news and to tell them there would be workshops on how to write a resume, interviewing best practices, and how to conduct an effective job search.

The one person I remember was William. William came in and was obviously suppressing his anger. He was breathing deeply to control himself.

He blurted out, "They didn't have the guts to tell me about my performance and used economic circumstances as an excuse to let me go."

William continued, "I sensed a long time ago that my manager was not pleased with my performance. I tried three times to identify the problems. I asked him how I could improve. I received no feedback. It was obvious he was uncomfortable and wanted the conversation to end.

"So I repeat, the manager didn't have the guts to tell me what I needed to do to improve." William was shaking his head. "It's bad enough to lose a job but it's worse to not know why. If I knew why I was let go, I wouldn't make the same mistake next time."

William's "He didn't have the guts" comment motivated me to find the best way to conduct a performance improvement conversation. Let me demonstrate what I learned in a role-play. My role is to be the new manager and your role is to be William.

Here I go as the manager: "William, your performance is less than satisfactory. We need to improve that. Consequently, I picked two job-related goals for improvement. I also picked two areas for interpersonal development. These will be your development plan."

In my role as the manager, I will then go over William's development plan, listening to see if he's receptive and takes responsibility to improve.

I will ask for questions and after answering them, I'd say, "William, often an emotional message isn't heard. Use me as a resource. Can you think of anything I can do?"

Then I would say, "Here are the next steps. We will meet weekly to review your progress and answer questions."

Let's assume after four weeks William's performance has not improved.

"William, you are not meeting our expectations. This cannot continue. Your behavior in the next two weeks will tell me if you can perform your job. I want to be clear, if you cannot do your job here you will be looking elsewhere. Again, I'll help, just ask."

MANAGER TAKEAWAYS:

- Concern for others is required. You have a duty to tell people about performance concerns. (Caution—don't be so indirect they never get the message.)

- The desired outcome is that they learn and improve so the company doesn't have to go through a job search.

- They get a second chance.

- Losing an employee translates into significant cost, lost time and disruption of the relationships.

APPENDIX:
The Tool Kit

The following seven appendix sections are tools in my tool kit that I like to share with my coaching clients.

A. **You Don't Have to Take It Personally**

B. **Improve Relationships**

C. **Best Practices: Delegation**

D. **Quick Supervisor Update Report**

E. **Think Like a Consultant**

F. **Change a Habit**

APPENDIX A

You Don't Have to Take it Personally

The first tool to use so you don't take it personally is an analysis.

Reasons why, when I'm in my head, I take it personally:

- I am my brain.

- My brain contains my ideas.

- My ideas and my brain are my identity.

- That is who I am.

- When you question or challenge my ideas, you are threatening or attacking who I am.

- If my ideas are questioned, then I'm not performing.

- Who I am is in question and security is threatened.

- The more I feel attacked, the more I will retreat to my island of me, or I will lash out.

Improved perspective is to realize I'm more than what I think.

Analysis of why, when I'm in my emotions, I take it personally.

I've told myself a story about the other person.

1. **Alternatives**—Put the story I made up aside. What are the alternative ways to view the situation? Is it possible I had a role in creating the condition?

2. **Evidence**—Where is the evidence that this is true? What facts do I have that the other person is (my assumption)? Go for objectivity.

3. **Implications**—If part of my story is true, what are the implications? By looking at the implications I will be in a better position to take positive action.

4. **Usefulness**—How useful is my story? How useful is it to believe (my assumption)? Even if the story is true, or mostly true, how useful is it if it leads to suboptimal results?

Improved perspective is to realize I'm telling myself stories.

APPENDIX B
Improve Relationships

Here is how to improve relationships. First, find common ground, which means to understand what they want and need.

Also, find common ground in your personal life. Keep in mind there are very real rewards when relationships are working. Strong relationships can put people at ease, open the door for the truth, speed up outcomes and keep things from escalating.

Here are my top ten tips:

1. **Don't be seen as competitive.**
   Generate possibilities rather than staking out territory or a position. Also be more tentative and open. Emphasize common goals and problems. Invite criticism with something like, "Why won't this idea work?"

2. **Win some, lose some.**
   Try not to be too good at winning them all. If you are seen as willing to lose for the good of others, others will return the favor.

3. **Self-monitor.**
   How often do you take a stand? How often do you make an accommodation statement? What is more important to you: the relationship or the issue? Anticipate stressful situations and rehearse your answers.

4. **Respect the position.**

Separate the people from the problem, i.e., don't get personal. Respect means not being seen as pushing something on them. Understand their position. Ask a lot of questions before you state your side of the case.

5. **Think laterally.**

Be aware that the least-used flow in an organization is lateral exchanges of information and resources.

6. **Others influence promotions.**

Never forget that.

7. **Problems with someone?**

Avoid telling others. Go to the person directly and resolve it. If you are quiet, you are the problem. They can't read minds. Practice beforehand.

8. **Influencing without power can come from understanding, which comes from questions.**

What do they need from you? How does what you do affect them? If there is a negative effect you can't avoid, is there a trade? Is there a common good to be achieved?

9. **Are you turned off by them?**

Find the good and get over it.

10. **Seek help.**

If there is a maze you can't figure out, get help from people who are good at picking their way through the confusion.

APPENDIX C

Best Practices: Delegation

••

Make Yourself Let Go

As a manager/leader, move beyond, "It's faster if I do it" and "I know more than they do."

- To "let go" means to build trust and relationships.

- To "let go" means to build skills and bench strength.

- To "let go" is to not control another.

- To "let go" is to allow learning from consequences.

- To "let go" means to check periodically and not to abandon.

- To "let go" is to let them make the most of the opportunity.

- To "let go" is to provide the "what," then let them decide the "how." (If they don't know "how" then teach them.)

- To "let go" is a vote of confidence.

- To "let go" is to let your ego die.

- To "let go" is to paint a picture of what they can become.

- To "let go" is to fear less and trust more.

Ask, Don't Tell

- What do you think should be done?

- What do you think led to this problem?

- What are the pluses and then minuses of what you are proposing?

- How have others handled this in the past?

- How will this affect others in the company?

Why Delegate?

You gain time to think, have shorter hours, and accomplish more. Delegation motivates others and gives them a chance to develop. Tip: Don't just delegate the "junk" stuff.

Why is Delegation Often Ineffective?

One of the most common problems with delegation is incomplete or cryptic up-front communication which leads to frustration, a job not well done the first time, rework, and a reluctance to delegate next time. Poor communication and being rushed costs you more time later.

How Do You Delegate, Save Time, and Ensure Results?

Replicate these eight steps below with spaces to fill in and then give them a copy to fill out as you discuss the project. Request a filled-out copy for yourself. Also, if someone is delegating a project to you, pull out the eight steps and fill in the blanks.

1. What does the outcome look like?

2. When do you need it by?

3. What's the budget?

4. What resources do they get? (Link them to the people and resources they need, such as, "You need to talk to...")

5. What decisions can they make?

6. What decisions do they need to check with you on?

7. Do you want checkpoints along the way? (You should have some.)

8. How will we both know and measure how well the task is done? (Be specific.)

More What and Why, Less How

The best delegators are crystal clear on what and when and more flexible on how. People are more motivated when they can determine the how for themselves. Inexperienced delegators include the how, which turns the people into task automatons instead of an empowered and energized staff.

What to Delegate?

Delegate as much as you can, along with the authority to do it. Delegate more whole tasks than pieces and parts. People are more motivated by complete tasks. A good question to ask: What do I do that you could help me with? What do I do that you could do with a little help from me? What do I do that you could do by yourself? What do you do that I could do faster and more effectively?

Whom to Delegate to?

To those who can do it and those who can almost do it. If they can't do it, is it because they don't have the aptitude? Is it because of lack of training?

How Can You Cultivate Independent Thinking?

Ask them to think in terms of rating their problems.

1. A one means the manager solves the problem.

2. A two means the manager tells you how to solve it and you follow up.

3. A three means you propose a solution and ask for the manager's approval.

4. A four means you take action and tell the manager afterward.

The goal is to rate as many problems as possible as a four.

APPENDIX D

Quick Supervisor Update Report

Goal: Five Minutes to Read and Fifteen Minutes to Prepare

We the bosses can ask our direct reports to provide us with a quick report. Make sure point numbers 1, 2, and 3 below are your key drivers. Once you have done that, they now know your expectations. It's an open book test. You can monitor the results and then, as point number 4 suggests, you will invest in their improvement. The report isn't an "I got you." It is an "I want you to know how you are doing" report.

We the direct reports assume the boss knows what we do. Generally, this is wrong. The boss usually knows only 20 to 30 percent of what you are doing. Regardless of the percentages, it helps to keep the boss informed. Accomplishing the items in the lists below directly correlate with your salary increases, promotions, and job security.

Action Steps:

Write a quick report each week that:

- is no more than five minutes to read
- takes no more than fifteen minutes to write
- is limited to one half-page or less

- contains bulleted information that identifies what you've actually done in the past week and fits into four categories (you may want to leave these examples of categories alone, change categories, or ask the boss for his key drivers)

1. How I made the company money this week.

2. How I saved the company money this week.

3. The crisis I prevented this week.

4. Areas where I can use the boss's/reports'/partners' help in getting something done.

APPENDIX E
Think Like a Consultant

....

This tool is useful if you want to think like an external consultant. It is how to create a conceptual agreement.

A great way to prevent frustration is to know what your internal or external clients really want.

Scan this list and see if there is an application. If there is, then pare the list down to fit your circumstances.

1. **Agreement on the objectives to be met.**
   This point answers questions such as:

   - What would you like to change, fix, or improve the most?

   - How would things be different from now at the conclusion of our three sessions?

2. **Agreement on what measures will be used to gauge progress.**
   Answers questions such as:

   - What is the range of improvement you'd like to see, what is the minimally acceptable, and what represents overwhelming success?

   - How would you know these outcomes have been achieved?

3. Agreement on what the value of achieving this will be to the company.

Answers questions such as:

- What will the outcomes mean to you? To your career? To the company?

- What does this mean quantitatively (sales, market share, profit, retention, etc.)?

- What does this mean qualitatively (attracting the best people, health, reduced stress, reputation, comfort, ego, etc.)?

Be patient—they often are not sure what they want, so help them, even if they are in a hurry.

APPENDIX F

Change a Habit

···

Here are my percentage guidelines if you want to change a habit:

- You're 6 percent on your way by pausing, thinking about what you want to improve along with the benefits to you and others.

- You're 20 percent there when you write down your goals and the barriers.

- You reach 60 percent by telling others the observable old behaviors and the new improved behaviors. Think about the Pareto Principle, also known as the 80/20 rule. An example of a good mental note: "I over-talk and the spotlight is on me 80 percent of the time. You will now see me talking 20 percent of the time and listening 80 percent. The bottom line: It's about them, not me."

- You hit 85 percent when you ask others to be your partners in change. You repeat the old observable behaviors you want to stop and the new behaviors you want to start.

Think about the dynamics of inviting others to help you. You are not putting them on the spot because you identified what you want to change.

You are modeling for others an openness and willingness to change. Ideally, they will ask you to do the same for them; or if they don't ask, offer to help them just as they are helping you.

Acknowledgements

What we think is what we become. Think you can improve your work life, and you can. This may surprise you, but you can do it one conversation at a time. You've read how others removed their frustrations through conversations. Follow in their footsteps.

A guide and a standard to apply: "Don't become so well-adjusted to your culture that you fit into it without even thinking."

The quotation inspired me to challenge myself and others to stop being passive, start thinking differently, and redeem what you've lost at work.

My *do something* was to write a book so you can make a difference in even the most dysfunctional circumstances by changing the way you think and react to your situation.

Please treat yourself as if you are already what you can become, then treat others as if they are already what they can become.

A partial list of encouragers I wish to thank are:

Jill Porter
Bill Enns
Bob Snigaroff
Bruce Elliott
George Kenney
Kai Adler
Henry DeVries
Katherine Ragusa
Rick Ragusa
Sue Bunnell
Art Miley
Bette Hansen
Clyde Hansen

Neal Nordstrom
Hope Carlson/Chen
Morgan Miller
Tim Bubnack
Paul Kim
Hunter Benson
Eric Kapur
David Baldwin
David Levy
Michael Corbett
Mark Porter
Rick Egan
Devin DeVries

About the Author

Kent Porter has logged 10,000 hours of coaching conversations spanning twenty years.

In an earlier career with a multinational company, he progressed from sales to VP of Sales to Executive VP to CEO of a subsidiary company he founded.

He left the corporate life to bootstrap a business to 110 employees in five states. After fourteen years, he closed the business and went in search of what he could have done better.

This was the beginning of a leadership development and coaching consultancy. He had corporate and entrepreneurial experience but lacked rigorous training in coaching, which he then acquired at the Center for Creative Leadership (CCL).

He is a graduate of the Thunderbird School of Global Management and the University of Kansas. He is proficient in Spanish and conversant in Portuguese. He is a Board Certified Coach.

Made in the USA
Charleston, SC
29 August 2016